Changing Gears:
Entrepreneurs @ 50+

Dr Angela C. Robertson

Changing Gears:
Entrepreneurs @ 50+

Paradise Publishing

ISBN: 978-0-9911941-0-7

Cover Image:
Steven Novak
Novakillustrations.com

Books by the same author

The *'Older and Bolder'* series

Available from your favourite online bookstores in paperback, Kindle,
and e-Book formats

Life on Our Own Terms

Celebrating Life on Our Own Terms

Embracing Life on Our Own Terms

Creating Life on Our Own Terms

Dr Angela C Robertson (books2read.com)

Want to be kept up to date with new books, information, and
speaking engagements? If so, email me to register your interest
and be one of the first to find out about new releases.

Kiaora@angelarobertson.nz

For more information and details of events check out my website

www.angelarobertson.nz

CONTENTS

Preface

The idea for this book came from chatting with dozens of men and women in New Zealand, who, for one reason or another, chose to start a business aged 50+. It takes courage, fortitude, and a tolerance for risk to become an entrepreneur at any age. Whilst most of us want flexibility and autonomy in our work, setting up and operating a business requires a high degree of confidence and enthusiasm, a wide range of skills, is time consuming, and is generally harder than working for someone else. Nevertheless, there is an emerging trend for people to start a business for the first time in later life, and this has increased since the onset of the COVID-19 pandemic. According to the Office for Seniors, self-employment income for older people is projected to increase from $3.98 billion in 2021 to an incredible $17.19 billion by 2071. Why do individuals in the second half of life choose to change gears, and go down this route? What is the trigger? What motivates them? What is the nature of the businesses they establish, and how do they go about it?

Entrepreneurs in the second half of life, challenge the stereotypical belief, that advancing age narrows down life choices. It doesn't! These individuals create their own reality, often seeking a different career path with more meaning. We all love stories and can learn from other people's experiences. It's with a deep sense of gratitude that I share the stories of 33 entrepreneurs at 50+ in this book, and my own experience. Their businesses range from the conventional to the 'out there', and their experiences include candid accounts of the challenges they faced, and their aspirations for the future.

Regardless of our age and stage, circumstances and experiences, there are always opportunities to pick up ideas and lessons learned from others who have embarked on this path in the second half of adult life. And, if you have that nagging feeling of 'what's next for me', inspired by their example, you might like to 'give it a go' too!

"There is no greater thing you can do with your life and your work than follow your passions – in a way that serves the world and you."

Richard Branson

Introduction

New Zealand is a nation of small and micro businesses - representing an incredible 97% of the total number of firms. In this country, small businesses are defined as having fewer than 20 employees and include the self-employed. To provide perspective, this equates to approximately 530,000 small businesses, of which 410,109 (76%) are managed and operated by the self-employed (solopreneurs). These businesses account for 28% of the nation's employment and contribute to more than 25% of New Zealand's gross domestic product (GDP).

What's more, 45% of the self-employed, self-starters in New Zealand – let's call them 'Entrepreneurs', are over the age of 50 (**10 Facts About Small Businesses in New Zealand | Small Business Blog (bizcover.co.nz)**). Clearly solo entrepreneurs, and small businesses are an integral part of Aotearoa's thriving economy. Who are these people? Why did they start these businesses – what is their motivation? And what kind of businesses are they in? Read on!

The exciting thing is, as the population is ageing, these numbers are expected to grow **May 2022 | Te Tari Kaumātua (officeforseniors.govt.nz)**. Globally, people are not only living longer **World Population Ageing 2019: Highlights (un.org)**, but they also want to be active for longer, stay healthier for longer, and engage with their communities for longer. And many of us want a longer working life. There is a huge segment of the population that has the potential to use their later working years contributing to the greater good in all kinds of ways. We want to make use of our accumulated skills and experiences, accomplish new things, and some of us are very creative in the way that we go about this. A third of New Zealand's workforce is over the age of 50, and greater numbers of people over the age of 65 are choosing to remain in the workplace for social and economic reasons. But unfortunately, age discrimination is endemic in our society. Employers often don't consider older adults for some roles or are concerned that they either can't learn new skills or are not prepared to train them. Consequently, it can be challenging for people over the age of 50 to get a job and remain in fulfilling work that: -

- Meets their needs and aspirations,
- Utilises, and leverages their skills, and experience,
- Maximises their potential, and,
- Supports their overall wellbeing.

And then there are those who are disadvantaged through the effects of gender, ethnicity and/or disability (Older-Workers-Action-Plan-FINAL.pdf (officeforseniors.govt.nz))

For many, mid-life is a time for reflection. It's one of those stages in life when we take stock of what we've experienced to date, what we've achieved, and who and what is important to us. This was magnified with the impact of the COVID pandemic: The uncertainty of life, renewed focus on overall wellbeing, swings in the economy, grappling with multiple lockdowns, the divisiveness in families, communities, and workplaces between the vaccinated and the unvaccinated, restrictions on domestic and international travel, new ways of working from the comfort of home, thus eliminating the need for long, stressful, and expensive commutes, and with that the change in personal, family, and financial circumstances. We are even more mindful of what has gone before, acutely aware of the present, and speculate about the future.

It's liberating to realise we can take control and change gears at any age if we want to. After all, life is a continuous adventure, chronological age is just a number, a state of mind, it's our functional age that matters. While everyone's perspective is different, in our 40's 50's, 60's, 70's, and 80's, we are smart, productive, and want to make a difference. Considering the future, the word 'retirement' in the traditional sense, at any particular age, doesn't resonate with many individuals. We come to realise that we can reconsider our options, unleash our potential, learn new skills, expand our horizons, and navigate a new reality at any age if we want to.

The day I left my substantive job I entered a new stage of active life. It's been a journey of personal development, growth, and empowerment, resulting in a flexible, balanced lifestyle, reconnection with the community and a focus on purposeful activities. And I'm not alone. Every year, thousands of others around the globe embark on a similar journey, each navigating their own route to re-ignite their lives, explore, and/or develop their passion, re-charge their batteries, search for opportunities, and find another way of leveraging their talents, contribute to the community, and earn a living.

In this book, I'll introduce you to 33 entrepreneurs. These are real people over the age of 50, from all walks of life, who have taken a risk, established a business in New Zealand, from which, they are creating a stream of income. Some service the domestic market, others are operating on a global scale. Note that this is not an academic book with detailed references and financial statements. It's a collection of cameo short stories about everyday people, just like you and me, who became single or multi business owner operators - some unexpectedly. Most of these individuals had never thought of themselves as entrepreneurs – but they are. And now they are living the dream, generating an income while crafting a life of independence and purpose.

There is seldom an isolated reason why people change gears, let go of established careers, and start businesses in mid-life and beyond. There are usually a combination of factors or triggers that set individuals off along this route. After all, everything is connected. Making the decision to set up a business, launching it, and managing the day-to-day operation, can be very challenging steps to take. While many people dream of starting a business, and may have excellent ideas for starting one, not all get around to translating their dreams and ideas into action – especially if this is a new idea or experience after many years in a corporate or industrial environment.

Whatever your age and stage, overcoming the scary fear of the unknown may be one of the biggest hurdles to overcome. Self-doubt is another. Let's face it, when we were younger, we may have been more inclined to take risks. We knew if we made mistakes, and things didn't work out, we could handle it as we had plenty of time to try something else.

The mindset is different in mid-life and beyond. We have a work history; we've put energy into developing a career – or maybe several careers. We may have purchased a home, had a family of our own, travelled, and saved for our retirement. With decades of life experience, we have encountered highs and lows in one way or another. Moving into the second half of life, it's natural to want to protect what we've accumulated. We want certainty, the security of the known, rather than the uncertainty of the unfamiliar. Although we may have brilliant ideas for a business, and the skills and enthusiasm to make it work, we may be more hesitant to let go of what we've studied for, worked hard for, and accomplished to date. Over the decades, we've developed familiar routines, forged relationships with colleagues and friends, many of whom we may have known for years, and countless others have built a network of relationships in an industry related field. Though we may yearn for the freedom to start a business, it may be hard to step out of our comfort zone to give something else a go.

On the other hand, we may also feel trapped in the status quo, on a treadmill, doing the same thing, day-in-day-out, having the same conversations, with the same people, resulting in the same outcomes, and ask ourselves, "Is this it"?

What about those who find themselves burnt-out, in a rut or facing unanticipated redundancy? There are some who are desperate to retire from a particular job, but not retire in the traditional sense.

Then there are those among us who experience an earth-shattering life event such as a serious illness, the bereavement of a significant other, or a divorce. In these circumstances, individuals, and their close family members, suddenly find themselves making multiple changes in their lives.

Some people become accidental entrepreneurs. These are people who never in a million years thought they'd be running their own business, but due to a change in circumstances, they head down this track. In contrast, there are those who plan for years, are very clear on their goals and want to change gears and start a business to: -

- Fulfil a long-standing ambition,

- Follow a passion,
- Tap into their creativity,
- Make the most of the opportunities available to them to be their own boss,
- Live a flexible, balanced, lifestyle, and
- Create a stream of income to supplement their superannuation into the foreseeable future.

I'll introduce you to entrepreneurs, who, with a sense of renewal and enthusiasm, have experienced and overcome some of the identified hurdles.

In this book, we'll explore: -

- The nature of their businesses,
- Why these individuals chose to go down this route rather than remain in paid employment elsewhere,
- How they started their business,
- The major challenges they encountered, and,
- Their aspirations for the future.

Along the way, I'll share my own story. And for those who are toying with the idea of starting a business in the second half of life, encouragement, ideas, examples and tips, and links to useful websites and templates have been included.

The businesses that feature in this book range from the conventional to the 'out there'. While some of these entrepreneurs service the domestic market, others have multinational, business, aspirations, and goals. Regardless of your age and stage, circumstances and experiences, there are always opportunities to pick up ideas and lessons learned from others who have embarked on this path in the second half of adult life.

Note that this book does not focus on finance, how to get a

business loan, how to make millions of dollars, or get rich quick schemes. Everyone's personal circumstances and motivation is different, and later life is not the time to invest heavily or get into debt.

If you are wondering 'what next', have a business idea, want to pursue your passion, fulfil a long-standing ambition, take responsibility for your own destiny, and create a stream of income in later life, I hope this book inspires you to explore the possibilities and take massive action. I believe life is a continuous adventure. It's never too late to change gears, make bold decisions, take on new challenges, learn and implement new skills and take calculated risks.

2. Why do People Start a Business?

Some individuals are destined to become entrepreneurs, especially those whose parents or family members were entrepreneurs. These role models can be a great source of inspiration, encouragement and offer practical support. However, most, but not all baby boomers (those born between 1946-1964), tended to follow the more traditional track; leave school, train for a trade or a profession, and/or seek tertiary qualifications to fulfil our ambitions. Ultimately, most of us aimed to get a job – preferably one in an environment that we would enjoy, that paid well, and if we were lucky, offered ongoing training and career progression. Regardless of the route, the primary aim for most of us was to seek suitable employment, that provided a source of income.

The flexibility to pursue a passion, make a difference in the world, work our own hours, create something from scratch – a product or service, build a brand, create an asset, work from home – or from anywhere, are among the myriad of reasons why people start businesses today. But aspirations such as these were practically unheard of or regarded as unrealistic in the mid-late 60's, 70's and 80's when we were in our teens, or even in our 20's and 30s. While some individuals famously broke away from the long-standing traditions, in the post-World War II era, despite the increased birth rate and significant social and economic change, most of us pursued the long standing, time-honoured, conventional track. And, as the years rolled by, we established a work history. Traditionally, couples started a family, and with that accumulated financial responsibilities. I'm generalising, and recognise there are exceptions, but this was the trajectory many of us took, given the context of the time.

Over the decades, the concept of a 'job for life' until 'retirement', that offered stability and annual increments, has long since been eroded. It seems inconceivable now that this system ever even existed. In today's world, no job is guaranteed for life. These days individuals are more discerning about what they do for a living and often seek flexible ways of working depending on their interests, aspirations, and circumstances. Despite recurring shifts in the economy and immense social, cultural, and rapidly evolving technological change, people tend to be more mobile, and change jobs, careers, companies, and sectors with much greater frequency than our predecessors. As the population in most countries, including New Zealand, are living longer healthier lives, perspectives, and priorities about the second half of life and work are changing, and new trends are emerging. Not only are people choosing to remain in work for longer - often past the age of entitlement to superannuation, but there is also an increase in entrepreneurial activity in those who are 50+ across the globe.

So why do individuals in New Zealand start a business over the age of 50? What is the motivation that propels them forward to achieve their goals? As discussed, there is rarely an isolated reason why people change gears and embark on entrepreneurial activity in mid-life and beyond, but there is usually a trigger – a spark that sets off a chain of events. This could be as simple as a conversation, an experience or a set of circumstances that initiates an idea and a change of direction and stimulates the motivation to do something about it.

Without exception, all the entrepreneurs I interviewed for this book experienced a period of upheaval. Each of them identified a ***trigger***, or a series of factors that led them to pursue a new direction in life and identify their: -

- ***WHY*** – the compelling reason for starting a business in the first place. If business owners don't know why they do what they do, how will anyone else?
- ***WHAT*** – the nature of the business (products and services), and how they will be provided.
- ***HOW*** – the steps they took to get their business off the ground.

Considering their responses, four key themes emerged as to why they changed gears in the second half of life: -

1. A Life Changing Experience,
2. Responding to a Health Condition,
3. Mid-life Reflection,
4. An idea, a gap or an opportunity was identified, and they knew they could respond.

In the following four chapters, based on these themes, I'll share a snapshot of these businesses and the learning journeys of the people concerned. You'll gain insight into their ideas, perspectives, and their compelling desire to take massive action.

It's important to note, that while the motivation for most entrepreneurs is to generate an income, the motive for social entrepreneurs is different. Social entrepreneurs aim to make a difference, to help meet community needs and strengthen connections, and/or solve social problems. While they generate a stream of income, money isn't the primary motive for social entrepreneurs, and they don't necessarily expect to earn big bucks. Nevertheless, most entrepreneurs want to make a positive impact and make a living.

Whenever we take up a new pursuit, whether it's a sport, hobby, health regime, project, occupation, or start a business from scratch, it requires significant effort, persistence, and momentum to make things happen. In Chapter Six, we'll briefly explore the importance of mindset to achieve success. We'll also pinpoint the common fears we experience when we step outside our comfort zone, and how to overcome them.

Inevitably business owners face challenges – some are predictable, others take us by surprise. In Chapter Seven we'll discuss the key trials and tribulations these entrepreneurs encountered, and offer tips and techniques for managing these challenges, and minimising the risks and the anxiety associated with them. Links to useful websites and templates are provided.

It would be remiss to ignore the impact of COVID-19, especially as post the early stages of the pandemic, there has been an increase in older people starting their own businesses, so this will be discussed in Chapter Eight.

We'll gain insight into the aspirations and future for these businesses in Chapter Nine, and for anyone thinking about starting a business in later life, these entrepreneurs share their advice.

The closing chapter provides a brief summary with acknowledgements entitled Afterthoughts.

At the back of this book, you'll find a Business Directory of the people who feature in this book with links to their business details.

3 A Life Changing Experience

A life changing experience includes an event, or a series of events, or exposure to circumstances (excluding health issues, which I'll address separately), that made a significant impact on the individuals concerned – either personally or financially, which in turn triggered a change in direction.

In this chapter, six entrepreneurs share the spark that prompted them to act – the trigger, or series of factors involved. They reveal their strong why – the reason that fueled their inspiration, motivation, and drive to start their business. Each of the business owner-operators briefly describe the nature of their venture. They also share a snapshot of how they got their business off the ground.

Let me introduce you to them.

Denise Carnihan – Helping Hand African Tours and Safaris

When Denise's son began a school project on his family roots, it was a revelation to learn that her grandfather was a native South African. Aged 14, Denise's grandfather came to New Zealand with the Merchant Navy, and later met and married her grandmother. Stunned by the news, and curious to know more, Denise spent months tracking down her South African relatives, who agreed to meet them. Her trip to South Africa was intended to be the trip of a lifetime. It turned out to be a life-changing experience.

In South Africa, Denise and her husband Chris stayed with her new-found family. "Immersed in the culture, we were the only pale skinned faces in this community, a novelty not previously experienced in this part of town", she said. Strong bonds were forged with family and friends, with promises to return when it was time for them to leave.

On this trip, Denise and Chris traveled further north and to the east, to explore this vast continent. They experienced the natural beauty of the landscape, a staggering array of wildlife, and the abundantly rich culture which varied from country to country. Absorbed in the culture, the traditions, and the nature of the people, they experienced the affluence, and were exposed to extreme poverty - especially in Kenya. It was a complete contrast to what they had ever experienced before and tugged at their heart strings.

Returning home, Denise went back to her job in the luxury car industry – but found it difficult to settle. The lifestyle seemed to be completely at odds with what the couple had been exposed to.

Two years later the couple kept their promise and returned to Africa. Embracing the diverse cultures, renewing her relationship with her family, and deepening relationships with the people they'd met in Kenya and Uganda, Denise knew she wanted to do something that made a difference. Her work in the luxury car industry was a far cry from what she was looking for, so she resigned from the role.

On another trip to Kenya, Denise undertook voluntary work and came to the decision to start a school in a slum. She and Chris found some land, signed the lease, funded it themselves and set to work to make it happen with the locals. In 2011, the school opened with 117 children, which rapidly increased to 300.

Spreading the word about her decision in New Zealand, Denise wrote a book about her experience (I Share My Heart With Africa - Carnihan, Denise | 9780473317249 | Amazon.com.au | Books). She set up a sponsorship scheme and opened a charity shop, manned by volunteers, with all the profits from these two ventures going to sustain the school. It was a steep learning curve. She invested a great deal of energy and time in her venture, and with support from her husband Chris, they garnered enthusiasm from friends and family, took risks and learned through trial and error. Undeterred when the school floundered, they learned from their mistakes, and opened a second school in Kenya.

Each time Denise returned home to New Zealand, it reinforced the notion that her heart was in Africa, and she wanted to share the experience more broadly with others. She had a very strong **WHY**.

Then came the idea, the **WHAT**. "Let's share our life changing experience with others. Let's bring other people out to Kenya, to experience the beauty of the landscape, the culture, the people and traditions, the wildlife, and show them the school. We'll provide real African experiences and adventures where guests are nurtured and cared for 24/7. On our trips people will go to places most tourists never go to. They'll meet people most traveler's never meet, and they will support and make a difference to the lives of the local people, local communities, and small local businesses".

Denise had no prior experience in the travel industry, but she did have a strong why, which fueled the passion, the energy, and the drive to make it happen, and she had the support of her husband Chris. Wasting no time, she researched what she needed to do to make her business come to life. She sourced skilled assistance to get her website up and running (Home (helpinghandafricatours.com) Focusing on her knowledge and experience, she developed an itinerary for a trip to Kenya, hired a local guide, started a database, and emailed everyone she knew to promote the trip. Within 24 hours, she had 52 responses, and her first tour was fully subscribed._Two weeks later, inspired with the response, she organised a second tour, this time to Uganda. Within weeks a third tour was scheduled. Fully committed, Denise wasn't afraid of putting in the hours. She personally went on all three African tours and proudly included the school she and her husband had established on each visit. With these three tours, Helping Hand African Tours and Safaris was up and running. This business provides their guests with a truly memorable, life changing experience, and everlasting friendships. Broadening her networks, and through word-of-mouth referrals, this business has gone from strength to strength.

Kareen Holland – Kd One Skincare and Cosmetics

Kareen earned plenty of work experience in various roles in New Zealand and overseas. Focusing on their careers, she and her husband started a family later than their peers, but when the relationship ended, she found herself a single parent in Australia. This life changing experience was the prompt to return to New Zealand, to be closer to family, and to 're-set' her life, starting from zero, in her 50's as a single mum.

With a young child to care for, Kareen was determined to make positive changes, step up to the challenge, and seize opportunities to achieve independence - her **WHY**. While working in the United Kingdom she thoroughly enjoyed and completed a course in Make-Up Artistry. Applying these skills, she had also worked with several politicians prior to going 'on air' and did the make up for personalities on 'Wheel of Fortune'. 'Fair Go', 'Sale of the Century', 'Telethon'. In addition, from time to time she worked in this capacity with the film industry and the arts, so she had the connections.

Using natural products, she started making her own cosmetics from home. "As a professional make-up artist, I had seen firsthand how many of the traditional products - formulated with chemicals, could affect the skin, causing redness, irritation, extreme dryness, and many other symptoms. If individuals suffered from eczema and psoriasis, these traditional products just made this worse". Experimenting, she initially manufactured five natural products, and soon opened a retail shop in Wellington with a business partner. Drawing on her skills and experience, she supplemented her income by doing freelance make-up artistry work for people prior to them going 'on camera'.

Learning from her experience, Kareen made the decision to go solo – to achieve her goal to be independent. She moved her manufacturing operation and shop to Tawa, where she also offered a range of beauty treatments and services to the local community. Highly motivated, she developed her brand, broadened her network locally and further afield, and developed her website (Organic Skincare | KD One New Zealand Natural Beauty)

Kareen's business rapidly expanded. She now manufactures an extensive range of natural and organic skincare products and a soothing medicinal range, all of which, are made in New Zealand using locally sourced natural ingredients, that are chemical free. Furthermore, Kareen has retail and wholesale arms to the business and provides beauty treatments for her customers – that get results.

Kareen took responsibility. She did her research, assessed her skills, focused her time and energy on developing natural products, and committed to making her goal happen. Her dedication to her family and business has reaped rewards. Kd One won the Retail Association Top Shop Award, Health, and Beauty category. As Kareen's production process is GMP certified (Good manufacturing practice certification), she is licensed to export her products to overseas markets.

It's a huge zero to success story for Kareen, and one for her to be immensely proud of.

Jeanie Morrison-Low – Kapiti Hearing – Audiology and Hearing Aid Clinic

Jeanie's from Scotland, and Larry is from California - Larry and Jeanie got married quite late in life. They met, by chance, in Tokyo at a St Andrews night ball; Jeanie was in Japan at that time for a few months on a Ministry of Culture scholarship, and Larry was the Executive Officer of the Marine Corps barracks in Yokosuka. Larry retired from the US Marines six months after they got married about a year later. Jeanie's first degree was in Anthropology and History of Art, but she mainly worked as an English and Japanese language teacher before she got married aged 38; and she had previously lived in Japan for several years before she met Larry. Larry worked as an IT project manager in South Korea and Japan, and they lived in both of those countries together with their two small sons. While there, they came to New Zealand on holiday to see some friends they had met in the US. These friends lived in Raumati, and Jeanie and Larry came several times to see them before buying a house in Kapiti, because they liked it so much. This was following 9/11, which was one of the factors that prompted them to sell their house in Washington D.C. and allowed them to buy in Kapiti.

However, to move to New Zealand and live in this house, they needed to have an occupation and qualification that met the requirements of the New Zealand essential skills list. Audiology was the second from the top of this list on the New Zealand Immigration website at that time (although a few months later, it changed to "florist"!) It was in order to come to live in this house in New Zealand that Jeanie applied to Auckland University to do a two-year Masters in Audiology. To be accepted into what is a very science-oriented profession, she had to study university prerequisites in physics, neuropsychology, biological neurology and so on – which she was able to do via various US universities which ran online courses. Studying late at night after the children were in bed, and in the morning while they were at kindergarten and primary school in South Korea and Japan, she eventually got accepted onto the master's course in 2005. Once the Masters in Audiology was completed in early 2007, there would be a further year of clinical practice (done at a clinic in Palmerston North), before a qualifying exam was passed.

Meanwhile, Larry worked for the Department of Labour in Wellington, and, while Jeanie studied in Auckland, he looked after both children, becoming "Mr Mom" and taking part in school fund-raising sausage-sizzles at the weekend. He also became involved in local Kapiti life, including the US Marines Trust, and the small museum commemorating their time in Paekākāriki during World War II.

"Being able to hear again, or to hear better, is a life-changing experience for people, who would otherwise become increasingly isolated in a hard-to-navigate world of sound", says Jeanie. "I really love this job, and the chance it has given me to be part of the Kāpiti community, while meeting so many different people. It is a health profession where you can really make a difference to people. Thank you to New Zealand Immigration for listing it!"

Through this major change in her life's trajectory, Jeanie found her life purpose; her "Ikigai" – a Japanese expression meaning something that is valuable to one's life and requires a certain amount of effort to pursue it. This was such an opportunity, and she loved - almost – every minute of it, (although not being apart from her family while studying). At 50 years of age, she graduated and spent a further 2-3 years commuting to and gaining work experience in an audiology clinic in Palmerston North.

In late 2009, Jeanie rented a room at a local Medical Centre in Raumati Beach, closer to home, and opened her own audiology and hearing aid practice, Kapiti Hearing Ltd. This is an independent, owner-operated clinic focused on patient-centred care. It offers a variety of hearing services, including diagnostic testing, and hearing aids. (www.kapitihearing.co.nz)

Jeanie's practice specialises in personalised patient care, provided by fully certified MNZAS audiologists, as well as hearing aid repairs and consumables. Tinnitus advice and referrals to specialists are also available. The district is spread along the Kāpiti Coast in a series of villages and townships and has a growing ageing population. When Jeanie realised that some of her patients could no longer drive between these villages, she opened a second practice in Waikanae. Both practices are fully equipped with one phone number reaching both locations. Both practices are extremely busy, and now Jeanie employs several staff.

This is an incredible story. Jeanie, with Larry's support, invested a great deal of time and money (as an overseas student) to study in Aotearoa and fulfil the requirements to move to New Zealand with their family – their goal. She seized the opportunity to re-train in a completely different field and discovered her "Ikigai". Now she and her family are servicing a large and growing segment of the district's population, are creating jobs, and are making a significant contribution to the economy.

Marie Hannan – Nepal-New Zealand Connection

Marie is no stranger to business. Many years ago, in partnership with another couple, she and her husband Neville established Kāpiti Cheeses. It took a couple of years to get the seven-day a week operation up and running, and soon Kāpiti Cheeses, a thriving business was winning prestigious awards. Years later, when the business was sold, Marie invested in the property market, which was quite lucrative. In her 50's, reflecting on what was important to her, Marie began to question her lifestyle. She discovered she wanted to do something purposeful and make a difference in the world – this was her trigger.

Marie made a life-changing courageous decision to work as a volunteer in Nepal for two years. Just like that, she packed a few belongings and travelled 12,000 kilometers to Damak in the province of Jhapa, in Nepal, (approximately two hours from the Indian border). Marie loved the Nepalese and enjoyed her voluntary role so much she stayed for four years and lived off her savings. During this time several non-government organisations (NGO's), came to Nepal to teach the women how to knit, felt, and make jewelry with the intention of being able to create a sustainable income. Unfortunately, tourists don't visit the villages, so these women couldn't sell what they had produced – they had no employment opportunities. Troubled by what she saw and the impact it had on the Nepalese villagers Marie had found a very strong **WHY**.

WHAT did she do? Marie created employment opportunities and a source of income for the villagers, by purchasing goods directly from the Nepalese women, importing them into New Zealand, and sold their goods on their behalf.

In her late 50's, back in New Zealand, energised with her ideas, she planned and self-funded her venture. Through her personal contacts, Marie purchased and air-freighted goods from Nepal to New Zealand and stored them in her garage. Buying a few folding tables Marie became a regular stall holder at markets in Ōtaki, Foxton, Sanson, Paraparaumu and Wellington. Open for business, people flocked to her stall to purchase her unique merchandise, especially the colourful garments made from hemp, cotton, and wool – for example hats, gloves and jackets made by the Nepalese with New Zealand wool.

When she turned 65, Marie cashed in her Kiwisaver superannuation savings, and opened a small shop in Kapiti. This was so successful she moved to bigger premises at Coastlands Parade. Marie is very clear on the purpose of her business and manages it on her own terms. She only employs people who have an affinity with the Nepalese and the products they create. In her words, "the shop is a treasure trove and is getting Nepal known". Marie also markets her stock on facebook (1) Nepal NZ Connection | Facebook) and continues to sell her products to her regulars at 'pop-up' stalls at the Martinborough Fair, World of Wearable Arts and the Waipukurau and Ōtaki markets.

Edmund Hillary had an affinity with the Nepalese. Hearing the news about Marie's venture, representatives from the Hillary Commission visited her shop and were inspired by what a single person can achieve when they put their mind to it.

Marie's life changing experience is an incredible story. She often shares her personal learning journey with community groups. Clearly, she demonstrates that age is no barrier to helping others, and through her business she leads a purposeful, productive, and fulfilling life.

Helen Hancox – No Nonsense Networker

Growing up, Helen's parents owned a bakery, "Although they worked the dough to make the bread, they never made much dough (money). Early on I saw that stressed, tired and grumpy is no way to live". Being in business was not for her, especially when there was a secure crop of jobs in the government sector. Her employment in this sector lasted for 16 years, followed by a couple of years as an assistant to an investor. In the late 1980's, her son Eric was born and suddenly through this life changing experience, she was out of the world of work to take care of her child. "My life and income changed. I spent the next 15 months on welfare".

Helen calls herself, 'an accidental entrepreneur'. Had she not had the life changing experience as a solo parent with a limited income, she may never have started a business. Turning this around gave her a very strong **WHY**.

Weaning herself off a social welfare benefit, Helen set up 'Flying Filing Squad Limited' – a records and management company specialising in the retention and disposal of government records. Assessing her transferrable knowledge and skill set she drew on her extensive administration experience in the sector "prior to sliding off the public service lifestyle". **WHAT** Helen's business offered was a range of services that addressed all of the 'pain points' in business.

HOW did she do it? Helen had a clear understanding of how the Public Service operated - the systems, processes, and the legislation. Armed with her knowledge and skills, she leveraged her expertise to help lots of businesses save time and money, by reviewing their retention and disposal records and schedules. In doing so, she helped them to identify and manage their inactive records and dispose of the ones that didn't need to be retained. She developed appropriate, workable, classification systems for the documents they did need to keep and ensured that records were listed to Archives New Zealand Standard. Who wouldn't want this service? Her business was a huge success. And what's more she could work her own hours, in her own way. The once reluctant entrepreneur was on a roll.

Helen's entrepreneurial experience expanded. In later life she has developed a highly profitable global online business that she operates from her home called 'No Nonsense Networker' (www.facebook.com/HelenGlenysHancox). She offers no nonsense support, tips and tools to small and medium businesses, so that people don't spend their time "spinning their wheels". Instead, Helen helps them to focus on making an impact. Helen practices what she preaches. She offers support to a selective group of people (both on and offshore), who are intent on growing their businesses. Helen audits Facebook profiles and advises people on how to turn their profile into a sales funnel. Learning from her experience she said, "At the end of the day, we all make choices. Accountability is the key".

Paul Streekstra – Bird Song Audio

Paul, an audio engineer and audio engineering teacher with the Music and Audio Institute of New Zealand, (MAINZ), enjoyed his job, which was focused on industry-related education in Auckland. But in his early 60's, his world turned upside down when the MAINZ faculty transferred from Tai Poutini Polytechnic to the Southern Institute of Technology.

Subsequently, a new structure was implemented, and Paul was made redundant. It was a huge blow at this stage of life, and a very stressful situation for him and his wife Lisa. This life changing experience was the trigger for them to make major lifestyle changes.

Reflecting on his passion, skills, and depth of experience Paul knew he could share his expertise in audio, music, broadcast, and advertising production more independently than he had before, working directly with musicians, advertisers, and the business community by providing professional guidance and services in his field of expertise – his **WHY**.

WHAT steps did Paul take? With his wife's support, he invested his redundancy package in audio and production equipment and set up his business, 'Bird Song Audio', in his home in Auckland (www.birdsongaudio.com)

The trigger, redundancy, and with that a change in lifestyle, prompted further discussion between Lisa and Paul. A series of decisions were swiftly made to renovate and sell their Auckland property and re-establish themselves closer to family in the Wellington region – which they did. In Paul's mind the options were limitless. Well known as, 'the studio guy', Paul had developed a strong track record in his professional fields. He's worked with musicians such as Dave Dobbyn and The Exponents and has recorded everything from voiceovers to orchestras. He'd also developed a network in advertising, radio, and corporate environments, and was quick to let them know about his new venture and offer his services.

It's widely known that being made redundant is an extremely stressful experience, especially if it occurs later in life as it did for Paul. But rather than focusing on the negative impact of this experience, Paul focused on his strengths and, together with Lisa, they made massive lifestyle changes and embraced the opportunity for a fresh start.

Whilst the nature of the events and circumstances for these entrepreneurs were all very different, the trigger that set them off on a journey of discovery and personal growth was a life changing experience. Making a big life change is scary, but with renewed energy these entrepreneurs found meaning and purpose – each found their "Ikigai".

4. Responding to a Health Condition

Some health conditions are indeed life-changing experiences, but this trigger sparks more than a change in direction. Usually unexpected, injury, illness and/or a diagnosis can be confrontational as we come to grips with our own mortality, and the blunt recognition that life is short. Injury, as a result of an accident, and chronic illness, can be physically and mentally debilitating, and a harrowing experience for family members. Hospitalisation, surgery, specialist treatment and day-to-day support may be required. Day-to-day activities are reprioritised. Domestic and workplace commitments, and financial responsibilities may need to be reviewed. Let's face it, serious health issues, and their treatment, have an impact on everyone in the family.

Starting a new venture in response to a health condition isn't typically a recipe for lowering stress levels. Therefore, the nature of the of business must be able to accommodate prevailing health issues and offer a degree of flexibility in the way in which they are initiated and operated. In this chapter, ten entrepreneurs – six individuals, a married couple and a mother and son duo share their respective stories. They all started a business after having experienced a chronic health issue or are living with a debilitating condition. Through their experience, they reveal their strong **WHY** that propelled them to take control of their destiny. They share the steps they took to get their venture off the ground, despite the challenges they faced regarding their own health and wellbeing.

Annette Burrell – The Inner Path

For years, Annette, was employed as a Team Leader of a group of therapists working with children with disabilities in Christchurch. It was a job she loved. But quite unexpectedly, everything changed. In mid-life, after her children had grown up and left home, multiple heath issues began to manifest, and life became more difficult. Triggered by the desire to identify and address the cause of her health issues, her chiropractor, suggested she might like to retrain. He offered Annette a pamphlet on 'The Journey' – "a cutting-edge transformation and healing method". Intrigued, Annette enrolled in a session to learn more about it. Inspired by the experience, she undertook a series of workshops, and went on to gain a qualification as a Journey Practitioner. "It was a transformational experience for me. I learned how to get in touch with specific emotions and applied the practice I had learned to myself and to others. I personally experienced the benefits".

Meanwhile, a series of earthquakes occurred in Christchurch. More than 180 people died, several thousand were injured, and the widespread damage impacted on health and wellbeing of the general population. In her mid-50's, with renewed energy, Annette recognised the need for additional support for the community. She said, "The training gave me the energy to cope, and the passion to help others to get to know their real self. I knew I could help these people" – this was Annette's **WHY**.

Taking control of her destiny, Annette reduced her working hours from five days to three. With the time she had freed up, she started her own private practice called 'Emotional Therapy'. Building on the foundational skills and experience she already had in psychology, sociology, and teaching, Annette offered advice and practical support to the community, and held one-day retreats for up to six-people on-site at her home. She created a labyrinth garden on her 2-acre section, which she used for meditation, and added a 'Journey Work' room for her therapy practice. In her business Annette provides one-on-one therapy sessions. She also leads relaxing one-hour meditations using crystal singing bowls (commonly known as Tibetan singing bowls), that can help heal mental and physical ailments.

Through her work experience, Annette had an established work history as a therapist, and an extensive network in her field in Christchurch, which she maintained. She wrote articles for the community newspapers, in which she shared advice, and offered practical support. As time passed, and she became more widely known in her field, she was a case-study for the Leela School. Since these early days she has continually invested in her development that includes, Neurolinguistic Programming, Emotional Inquiry and Clinical Hypnotherapy – all skills that support her practice.

Relocating to the North Island, she refreshed her business and website (The Inner Path | Be your true self | Feel alive and happy). Working from home, she offers a range of services to her clients, who are primarily women who range in age from their mid-30's upwards. She also facilitates one-day retreats at the Lotus Centre.

Richard Eltherington – Healthy Start (NZ) Ltd

Richard a family man, led an active, adventurous life, but everything changed in 2009 when he was diagnosed with cancer. "The diagnosis gave me a perspective on life. I had a family history - both of my parents prematurely died of the disease. I realised that life is too short. I knew it was time to do something else with mine". Following the diagnosis, he proactively sought treatment, and fortunately this was very successful. This was the trigger to make significant changes in this life.

Looking ahead, Richard developed a passion for health and wellbeing. Doing his research, he discovered that up to 15% of the planet had been affected by gut related problems, for example, irritable bowel syndrome (IBS), leaky gut, poor immune systems, lack of energy – and this was due to modern food processing and nutrition. Through his experience, and as a result of his research, Richard believes these problems can be avoided, and with that he had developed his compelling **WHY**.

In his early 50's, wanting to do something about it, Richard had found his purpose, and with the support of his family, they purchased a franchise to "Bring Natural Health Products to the World…..to benefit mankind".

Richard continued to do his homework. He sources and sub-contracts the manufacturing of the natural products in GMP (good manufacturing practice) certified factories in New Zealand, using natural ingredients with no chemicals or preservatives. "One ingredient we love to use is the famous New Zealand Manuka Honey", he said. Considerable investment has been made to develop and promote these products on the Healthy Start Group website. Richard also invested heavily in having a presence at trade and travel shows in New Zealand and overseas, including the Anaheim Natural Food Show in California, which attracts more than 20,000 companies.

The driving force has always been to grow this business from the start-up stage with a couple of natural products, and quickly move on to achieve the dream of a globally recognised brand with a full suite of natural body supplements. Richard said, "New Zealand is a small market – we had to go global". To do this, product compliance approvals had to be sought from the requisite authorities – no easy feat, but doable. To date, the Healthy Start group have distributors in New Zealand, Australia, Vietnam, and Russia. Richard is proud of the fact that, "All this is achieved from a small office in a seaside town in Aotearoa. We've worked hard to develop unique, natural, safe, and nutritious health supplements that help people feel their best inside and out".

Richard believes in and is passionate about his business and his products, he and his family use them every day. In his view, "Everyone should have the best life they can. Happy, healthy, and fulfilled".

Jules Fitzgerald – Tupperware Manager

For more than 30 years Jules enjoyed a corporate career in IT where she led a team of 18 people. Suddenly everything changed when in her early 50's, she had a crash on her bicycle, and suffered a mild traumatic brain injury, grazes, and bruises.

"Months of rehabilitation followed during which time I had lots of time to reflect. Six months later I had an epiphany moment. I knew it was time to make a change. I decided to take early retirement and take time out to heal. I had no partner or children and was financially secure – no mortgage and debt free. It was time for me to have fun. I took a leap of faith. The world of work grinds on, but I realised that no one is irreplaceable. It was hugely liberating when I handed my notice in. The worries fell off my shoulders".

As a young woman Jules had deferred her 'Overseas Experience' (OE), the New Zealand term for an extended overseas trip, to develop her career. "Recuperating from the accident was the perfect time for me to travel and detox", she said. When she regained her health, Jules travelled solo for nine weeks, experiencing her sense of adventure at her own pace.

Returning home, she was invited to a Tupperware party, which led to an invitation to become a consultant.

"Bored after a week of 'retirement' - I thought I'd give it a go. I would never have joined if I didn't believe in the goods. These are quality products with a lifetime warranty. I bought a starter kit and paid it off three Tupperware parties later. With support from the Director of Distribution, I soon became serious about it, and developed a plan of how I was going to do this. I worked to deliver on my plan, and found I loved it. That's when I made the decision, that I was in this for the long-haul".

Jules really enjoyed making personal sales and having the freedom to work with others. "I'm totally onboard with the products. I genuinely use them every day myself as I'm totally into reduce, reuse, and recycle. It's so easy to sell. Marketing resources are provided, but every consultant can put their own slant on it. I offer a personalised service and specialise in one-on-ones, or with two-to-three cooking in the kitchen. I look at what you can use in your pantry, fridge and freezer and come up with optimal solutions".

Jules travels anywhere to facilitate face-to-face parties. She also conducts online parties, which have been very successful, especially during the COVID lockdowns. "I always cook and give a hands-on demonstration. I provide the ingredients and the recipes, and we have a whole lot of fun. I offer kitchen storage solutions for fundraising parties, bridal showers, and baby showers. It's nothing like the old traditional way of doing Tupperware, where we all sat around – that's a thing of the past"!

Jules, who has been in this business for five years, is excited about her work. "I love the flexibility of working my own hours and being able to take care of my own wellbeing. I schedule my exercise and time to relax. I still enjoy recreational cycling, including long-distance events".

For Jules, the accident gave her the opportunity to step back and make a big change. It's one she has never regretted. She can be contacted by email julesfitzgerald4tupperware@gmail.com and on Facebook www.facebook.com/julia.fitzgerald.35

Genevieve McLachlan - dōTERRA Independent Wellness Advocate

Genevieve has cerebral palsy and low vision. An awesome individual, she takes personal responsibility for managing her physical and emotional wellbeing, can navigate potential challenges that come her way, and proactively develops her interests. When she accidentally tore a ligament in her hand, she sought traditional medical treatment, and also looked for natural alternatives to aid the healing process.

"I went to a class on essential oils. It was an enlightening education on how to make the oils, how to apply them, and the benefits of using them. I used a combination of five oils for 14 weeks while my hand was in a splint to help heal my muscle and joint issues. My hand therapist was very supportive and encouraged me to use the oils as well as doing the exercises. This worked so well for me, that I knew I wanted to develop an essential oils business so that others could experience the benefits as I had", she said.

Genevieve wanted to learn more about natural, environmentally friendly products, and where they came from. Doing her research, she was impressed with dōTERRA, an ethical company that sources essential oils from all over the world. dōTERRA works with partners to produce the purest, highest quality oils (Official Site of doTERRA New Zealand | dōTERRA Essential Oils) This company openly shared their research and implemented rigorous testing systems to ensure their products included no additives, a practice that resonated with Genevieve. "I bought a kit and got started. I experimented on myself, and when my family and friends became interested, I decided to move with it. I was 52 when I attended the training and went on to become an independent distributor". This became Genevieve's business.

Genevieve had already learned about the oils, and had sourced a supplier, but she recognised she needed help to boost her skills if she was going to make a go of her business. Researching what was available, she became one of the first people to go on the 'Elevate Programme', which "taught me everything I needed to know about being in business. I also worked with a mentor who helped me to get established".

Thirteen years later, Genevieve's business is thriving (1) Gen's Oils | Facebook) In addition to buying the oils and on-selling them to her customers, she focuses on teaching people how to use the essential oils to enhance their physical and mental health. "My teaching is based on experience. I share the success I've personally experienced myself, and the success I've seen working with others. I show people how to incorporate the use of essential oils into their daily lives".

Genevieve's story just goes to show what can be achieved when we put our mind to it.

Mark and Sone Edwards – Sone's Sauces

Ten years ago, Mark thoroughly enjoyed his job, as a chef at the New Zealand Police College, where he serviced the police recruits, the staff, and visitors to the premises. When a Thai delegation came to visit the College, the hospitality team planned the menu. They decided to offer a traditional authentic Thai meal, and enlisted Sone, Mark's Thai wife, to assist them to make it. They'd decided on a barbeque, and Sone made the salads and three Thai sauces from scratch using her own special recipes. The event was a huge success – the delegation loved it and commented on how wonderful the food was, especially the sauces. Encouraged by the feedback, Mark and Sone tried out their sauces on their friends, who then asked for bottles of the sauces to give as gifts to their families and friends.

Enthusiastic, Mark and Sone were keen to start a hobby business. Researching the requirements, they began to build a commercial kitchen on their property, to fulfil all the rules and regulations to get their venture off the ground.

Sadly, everything was put on hold when Sone was diagnosed with cancer. She was only 49. It was a very difficult time. The couple had four school-aged children, and Mark's job involved shift work. Sone underwent treatment, but her cancer spread over a three-year period. When another tumour was diagnosed, the prognosis wasn't good. Devastated, the family's world turned upside down. Sone, needed care, and Mark wanted to spend as much time with her and their family as he could. He resigned from his job. With no income, the building project, and plans for a business came to a grinding halt, and their lives were put on hold.

Time passed, more medical tests were undertaken, and to their astonishment, the original diagnosis proved to be incorrect - the second tumour was benign. It was such a relief. Although Sone was still very ill, and undergoing treatment, the couple began to look forward to a brighter future.

Mark and Sone revitalised their original plan. Their commercial kitchen was built in 2005, but it was upsetting for them to see it unused on their own property. Reflecting on their situation Sone said, "We wanted to do something with our lives. We wanted to leave our grandchildren something to be proud of, even if you can't do what you had intended to, you can still be successful". Mark said, "Sone wasn't well, and extremely tired, but we made our minds up to go into business, to make a go of it, and to do this together. Sone would make the sauces when she was well enough, and I would do the marketing".

They rolled their sleeves up, grew their own herbs, purchased the additional ingredients along with the jars and the packaging, and with that, the Thai sauce making production line began at their own pace. Their brand, their business skills and their website were developed over time, and a relative developed the label for their bottled sauces. (Home | Sone's Sauces (sonessauces.com)

"The great thing is, we found we were good at this stuff! We initially sold our sauces at the Martinborough Fair. We opened our stall at 8am and, encouraged people to do the taste test. We couldn't believe it. We sold all our stock – 300 bottles by 9.30am. We had a ball"!

Learning from their experience, Mark and Sone increased the volume of sauce they produced with the support of casual staff. They also made a deliberate decision to keep their range down to three products. "It's easier for people to make a decision to buy one, two or all three – the salad dressing, the satay sauce and the 'secret sauce' which can be used as a salad or pasta dressing or is nice with a Thai green curry".

Enjoying their experience, Mark, and Sone now sell their products and gift boxes to their regular customers at markets, large events, and trade fairs all over the North Island. Their sauces are also sold in wholesale and speciality grocery stores, selected supermarkets, delis, restaurants, and gastro pubs and can be purchased online directly from their website.

Mark and Sone's story shows that despite very challenging circumstances, business success is well within our reach. By refocusing on priorities, having a perspective on life and family, believing in yourself, and leveraging the knowledge and skills that you have, anything is achievable with a positive attitude and a commitment to make a go of it.

Suz Stokes – 35 Day Detox

Business owners Suz and her husband Ken spent a great deal of time living and working in Dubai. Whilst enjoyable, it was a hectic life, travelling and working in Southeast Asia and Middle Eastern countries, while juggling corporate activities in Australia and New Zealand.

By the time she approached her 50th birthday, Suz was exhausted. Around this time, she began to focus on a learning journey of physical healing and spiritual growth. Suz took up running, which later led to triathlon and endurance training, and yoga which led to Yoga Teacher Training. Investing in her spiritual growth, she studied astrology, numerology, feng shui, mindfulness, emotional fitness, physical fitness, and healthy whole foods. Revising her diet, she steadfastly used the gluten, dairy, and refined sugar free recipes she had been accumulating and sampling over the previous decade.

Meanwhile, Ken became extremely unwell, and returned to New Zealand. He was later diagnosed with cancer. It was evident their lifestyle had to change. Personal health and wellbeing became the focus – their **WHY**.

In a nutshell, Suz and Ken wound up their business affairs, and moved into their holiday home on the Kapiti Coast. Whilst Suz made a complete life change, she wasn't ready to retire. She also knew there were others out there who, like her, needed to reset the button on life. Drawing on her personal experience, her passion for wellbeing, and her experience in endurance sport, Suz founded a health and wellness company called '35 Day Detox'. Converting her garage into a private yoga studio, she leads individual and group yoga sessions and offers guidance on natural health and wellness in a business that she operates from home

Her research-based signature programme the 35 Day Detox Challenge is available online and includes an exclusive one-to-one consultation with Suz. She also offers personalized coaching services either in person, or online via Zoom. Suz's recipe book, which she personally uses on a daily basis, contains more than 100 natural recipes. "These natural recipes are specifically designed to create a happier, healthier you – manifesting change". Suz's recipe book is available as a PDF and as a hard back - check out her website for details (35 Day Detox - The

Natural Detox for YOUR Mind, Body & Soul)

Suz is not only passionate about wellbeing – she is dedicated to wellbeing. She walks the talk by taking a holistic approach to making changes in her own life.

In her book, *'The Physical Manifestation of Self – High Heels to Yoga Pants with a side of IRONMAN'* she tells her story of "arriving at the start line, being there at the end, and everything in between". It's available on Amazon in Kindle and paperback formats (The Physical Manifestation of Self: High Heels to Yoga Pants, with a side of IRONMAN : Stokes, Suz H: Amazon.com.au: Books)

Carol and Shaun Mahoney- Chirpy Plus

Carol spent her entire working life in technology and IT fields and was the first female Chief Technical Officer in New Zealand. Now in her 70's, she is very aware of the social challenges facing mature people like herself. Shaun, Carol's son, lives in Australia. He worked in the financial services industry, but his career path abruptly changed when he suffered a serious injury and underwent major surgery. Shaun spent a great deal of time in and out of hospital, and the lack of social interaction during his recovery had a profound effect on him.

Carol and Shaun both have cheerful, lively personalities. They are outgoing and are very people centred – but they realised, that what they had personally experienced was all too common. A disproportionate number of people aged 55+ feel disconnected and lonely, especially when they leave work, move to a new district, or become isolated for other reasons. While some people have lots of friends on Facebook, older people don't necessarily have the 'real life' personal connection they once had, and somewhere to go to meet people. This is not only occurring on both sides of the Tasman; loneliness is recognised as a global epidemic. The COVID-19 pandemic, with its numerous lockdowns and extensive social distancing regimes has compounded the problem.

Together, Carol and Shaun joined forces to do something about it. Their solution was to draw on their skills and experience, and develop a network in Australia and New Zealand, where people can connect with like-minded people in a safe environment. They explored several options and came up with the idea of 'Chirpy Plus' to help people connect. Chirpy's mission is to 'eliminate loneliness and social isolation in people aged 50 and over, by providing them with a safe and easy way to make new friends'. Fired up with enthusiasm Carol and Shaun tested the viability of their service by inviting foundation members of the network to join for free. The response was amazing – people seized the opportunity to belong. Chirpy Plus clearly met a need in the community on both sides of the Tasman, and for some people it was a lifeline.

The network that brings 'Chirpies' together face-to-face to meet new people and have fun together has rapidly expanded all over Australia and New Zealand. Hundreds of Chirpy group 'Catch up' meetings are taking place, each with a volunteer host who welcomes everyone, introduces people to one another, and helps facilitate the network meeting. Chirpies meet for brunches, walks, movie nights, factory tours, afternoons at the races and some even go on holiday together. To ensure people stay connected over the Christmas New Year holiday, Chirpy Christmas picnics are arranged for the members. Carol and Shaun recognised this is a time when people who live alone feel most vulnerable, and they have proactively done something about it.

This mother and son duo are passionate about their work. Carol manages the technology from her home in New Zealand, and Shaun manages the sales and marketing aspects of their venture from his home in Australia. They have no intention of setting up corporate offices for themselves or their staff and everyone loves the flexibility of this working arrangement. Check out their website www.ChirpyPlus.co.nz and www.ChirpyPlus.com.au

The service Chirpy Plus provides brings so much joy to thousands of people. Further expansion is on the horizon. Looking ahead, Carol and Shaun are planning to establish a Chirpy Plus network in the United States and the United Kingdom.

Retirement is not an option for Carol – she is living life to the max. She is proud of what she is achieving and likes being a role model, which proves age is no barrier to what you can do.

Tony Yuile – TY Coaching

Tony enjoyed a 30-year career in financial accounting and risk management in the Public Sector. But everything changed in his world when the organisation he worked for went through a lengthy structural review process. "For 12 months we went to work every day and waited for someone to make a decision about our future", Tony said.

Given the circumstances, stress and anxiety levels increased as the months rolled by, and then Tony began to experience pain in his right side. Seeking medical attention, he was relieved to hear that all the tests he undertook were negative. His problem was diagnosed as stress. Eventually the structural review was concluded, and Tony at 50 years of age, was made redundant. He recalls, "within three days of leaving my job, all my symptoms disappeared – just like magic".

Looking for a complete change in direction, a good friend recommended neuro linguistic programme (NLP) and hypnotherapy training with Richard Bolstad, (a Master Trainer with a Doctorate in Hypnotherapy). Completely outside his comfort zone, Tony enrolled in a new programme of development and applied his learning to himself. "It created a whole new level of awareness for me. I changed track from being a financial accountant and risk manager to become an NLP practitioner and went on to become an NLP Coach. I also studied hypnotherapy with the NZ School of Hypnotherapy, and now teach at this school myself".

Energised, Tony set up his own business as a Hypnotherapist, Life Coach and Hypnotherapy Coach (www.tycoaching.nz). Drawing on his personal experience, he specialises in dealing with stress, anxiety and more recently Irritable Bowel Syndrome (IBS) – the three areas he is passionate about (www.IBShypnotherapy.nz). Adopting an evidence-based approach, he offers courses, group sessions, and one-on-one coaching to "help people turn their lives around". Continuing his own education, he's been researching and studying these topics for the best part of a decade. In addition, Tony is a member of the global 'Your Life Live It' franchise, and in this capacity delivers three of their courses (Your Life Live It.com).

Tony is on a mission to "Put the power back where it belongs". He firmly believes "People can make choices – take control, and don't have to let others make choices for them". His book '7

Ways to Reduce Anxiety in 7 Minutes or Less' is available on Amazon in Kindle and paperback formats. (Amazon.com: 7 Ways To Reduce Anxiety In 7 Minutes Or Less: Think clearly, feel relaxed and perform at your best under pressure: 9780473353391: Yuile, Mr Tony: Books)

An accident or chronic health issue comes in many forms. A heath problem may develop over an extended period of time or hit you quite suddenly. Treatment may be brief, or ongoing.

There is nothing quite like a debilitating health issue to make you realise that your time is precious. The experience signals a change in direction and a sense of urgency in the search to find ways to: -

- Use your talents.
- Learn and apply new skills.
- Channel your energy into purposeful work that matches your energy levels and capability and earn a living.

Despite the curve balls these entrepreneurs experienced, they took advantage of the opportunities around them, and are now reaping the rewards.

As Napoleon Hill, author of 'Think and Grow Rich', once said,

"Our only limitations are the ones we set up in our own minds".

So true.

5 Mid-life Reflection

The interpretation of 'mid-life' or 'middle age' tends to vary from person to person. We may be in our 40's, 50's or 60+, depending on how you look at it. Regardless, in conversations with others you often hear people say, "I feel much younger than my age on the inside". We are as 'young or old' as we feel, and habitually act accordingly.

Accepting that we all age differently, and given the gift of healthier extended lifespans, it makes sense to embrace the ageing process, take good care of ourselves, enjoy life's pleasures, and make the most of the additional years later life offers.

Mid-life for many, is a time for reflection. It's one of those stages in life when we take stock of what we've experienced to date, what we've achieved, and who and what is important to us. We reflect on our lifestyles, routines, and our relationships. Working extended hours, it's so easy to get caught up in a constant state of busyness, or the pursuit of the next 'critical deadline', key performance indicator, sales target, or goal, aptly described by health and wellness coach, Nancy Weiser, as being, "like a hamster in a wheel on the route to corporate workaholism".

We want to ensure we have made the most of our lives, with few or no unfulfilled dreams, and no regrets. In the second stage of adult life, there is a sense of urgency to do what we want to do, rather than what anyone else wants us to do.

I'm reminded of a quote by Terence McKenna that I often heard in the workplace,

"If you don't have a plan, you become part of somebody's else's plan".

Thought provoking! The reality is that if we live life intentionally, we can change gears at any stage if we want to. In mid-life, when we contemplate the future it's possible to see the second half of life as the opportunity to re-vision and re-ignite our lives in one way or another. If we open our minds to the possibilities, and move out of our comfort zones, we can defy the stereotype that older adults are unwilling, or unable to embrace new ways of working.

In contrast we realise that we have accumulated a wealth of valuable experience, the ability to learn new skills, and can take advantage of the opportunities that are all around us.

Examples from ten entrepreneurs who took this step are shared in this section, which also includes a snapshot of my own story.

Andrew Burn – Enterprise Resource Planning

The trigger for Andrew was his 50th birthday. Reflecting on his life he asked himself, "What have I done? What have I liked doing? Is there something else I'd like to do? I spent my days doing things for other people and thought – 'what about me'. I realised that if you are successful, you should be enjoying it and be getting paid for it". This reflection prompted Andrew to take charge of his future. He invested in and completed an MBA and through the process he gained an invaluable understanding of business, 'managing in the moment' and teamwork. With this came an understanding of how he'd been perceived in his role. Stepping right out of his comfort zone, he went on an international study tour of India, specifically visiting Delhi and Mumbai - the biggest slum in the world. "It opened my eyes. It wasn't on my list of places to visit - a developing nation with 23+million people. It's so different to New Zealand. The scale of business was amazing, and the people were happy".

The study trip was the tipping point for Andrew. "I knew I'd changed. I realised I had the technical expertise (IT), to assist risk averse businesses with digital transformation. They experience a lot of fear and uncertainty when it comes to IT, and they don't know what to ask for – it's like 'The Emperor's New Clothes'". Andrew had found his **WHY**. "I had the people and the communication skills to identify and fully understand what the real barriers are for the people concerned. I knew I could offer them customised, integrated, systems to help these businesses move forward".

"I looked at my employer in a new way. I knew I had outgrown my job and the company, and I didn't want to work for someone else. It was time for me to move on. I wanted to work on a group of projects with people in the 'gig economy', by undertaking short term contracts and freelance work with businesses instead of having a job for life. ERP365 New Zealand was formed when I recognised that other partners were inflexible and uninterested. Often cloud solutions were implemented that caused disruption to business efficiencies. Customers wanted more. We help our clients remove barriers to growth, by introducing business process and automation, and leveraging digital disruption in a people-friendly way".

Andrew's **HOW** focused on establishing a niche in New Zealand - specifically the food importing, manufacturing, and distribution industry, which is huge. Using an integrated system that meets the specific needs of his clients, Andrew replaces the unworkable, stand-alone systems they had been previously offered. Utilising his MBA experience, he developed a website (erp365.nz). He also developed a marketing plan, which included direct marketing, the use of social media, and active networking, to create a presence in the marketplace.

In his business, Andrew has aligned himself with capable, skilled consultants, who share the same ethos, and has now built a strong brand. From his perspective, "It's all about quality". Now all the hard work is paying off, as his business is growing, especially through word-of-mouth referrals.

Cliff Gott – Secure Time

Cliff has enjoyed a varied career. As a young man he'd managed and operated a couple of businesses and had also worked in corporate environments for many years. In mid-life he and his wife relocated to the Kāpiti Coast, where like thousands of others, he commuted back and forth to Wellington. After four years, he was tired of the lengthy commute, which was a minimum of 20 hours per week. He also felt he'd outgrown the role he'd held for nearly 20 years, and he wanted more free time to enjoy life. Considering his future, he realised he much preferred being his own boss and doing his own thing. He also understood the nature of the community in which he lived and came up with his **WHY**.

"I'll provide services to people on the Coast that gives them back their time to enjoy life".

Reflecting on his skills and experience, Cliff determined **WHAT** - 'Your Time' would provide to residents in Paraparaumu and came up with three services: -

1. Lawn mowing – using eco-friendly tools he'd free up his customer's time and working outdoors was an opportunity for him to get fit.
2. Home security – fitting and servicing security alarms - a trade he had lots of experience in.
3. Handy time – providing handyman services tackling those small jobs around the home that his customers didn't have the time or the inclination to do.

Cliff was very clear on the parameters for his work, eliminating the commute, and to ensure he managed his workload and time.

Here's *HOW* Cliff established his business. "I did the research and identified the essential tools I needed for the job that were efficient, safe, and produced zero emissions into the atmosphere. I made the decision to purchase electrical gear which included my vehicle, which was my point of difference alongside similar businesses. I joined a couple of local networking groups and very quickly established my lawnmowing business through referrals". This strand of Cliff's business became his primary source of income, leaving little time to develop the other two elements of the business. He took on a casual staff member, Paul, another local entrepreneur, who needed the cash flow while he was in the process of establishing his own audio business in Kāpiti. It was a win/win situation for them both.

Cliff had originally intended to franchise 'Your Time', but within a couple of years, he came to realise the three strands he'd chosen, were incompatible with one another. Lawn mowing was weather dependent. The handyman work sometimes turned into much bigger jobs that took more time than had been anticipated. And by this time the security side of the business was beginning to pick up – but he was trying to fit this work in around the lawnmowing.

What's more, he found the security work was more interesting, more lucrative, and he was using his skills. Cliff decided to change gears. He sold his lawnmowing business to Paul – knowing his loyal customers were in good hands with someone they knew (another win/win situation see (Bird Song Lawn Mowing Service | Facebook). Cliff then focused his energy on establishing 'Secure Time' – his new business. He developed a new website (www.securetime.nz) purchased the necessary equipment and fitted out his new eco-friendly vehicle with excellent signage. He expanded his networking circle and began marketing the installation and maintenance of security alarms and CCTV systems on the Kapiti Coast. Within a few short months this business has gone from strength to strength.

Jan Thornborough – Cyber Resilience Intelligensia

In her role with the Government Communications Security Bureau (GCSB), Jan supported large organisations to protect themselves against cybercrime – a rapidly growing global problem. In her mid-50's, she became acutely aware of ageism in the workplace when she observed more and more people associating technological expertise with the younger generation. Then along came the COVID-19 pandemic. Increasingly Jan came to the realisation that, "In uncertain times, no job is secure, whether you are a contractor, or an employee".

Looking ahead, Jan wanted to continue to work in the longer term. She also wanted to fully utilise her skills and experience with the wider business community to make New Zealand a safer place for people to do business. Jan has no plans to retire at any specific age – after all, age is just a number and not an indication of functional ability and expertise – She had found her **WHY**.

Wanting to take control of her future, she decided to start her own business by offering "Cyber resilience services to small and medium sized businesses" – her **WHAT**. Drawing on her expertise Jan educates her client group on prevention, detection, and recovery from cyber-attacks. "In my experience conducting health checks and gap analysis, most businesses come up wanting. They rarely have everything in place. I make cyber security people practices, processes, and systems easy to do and appropriate for the size of the business".

So, let's find out **HOW** Jan got her business off the ground.

"Once I'd made the decision, I was honest and told my boss I was leaving. I got references and started developing my business processes while I was still in my substantive role. This included developing my website (Cyber Resilience | Intelligensia). I also designed, and implemented processes and developed my report templates, so that I wouldn't need to do this while marketing my business, building my client base, and providing the services to clients. I automated everything I could and invested in online tools upfront. I advised my networks that I was going solo, and the news swiftly spread by word of mouth. By doing this I was able to hit the ground running. Although it was unfortunate for those concerned, it was widely reported that a cyber-attack had a hugely detrimental impact on a cluster of hospitals, and this helped me to get customers. A high-profile attack makes people notice – before this people didn't take it seriously".

To promote her business Jan took the opportunity to present at conferences and events including The Institute of Directors, Chamber of Commerce, Entrepreneurs @ 50+ Network, Financial Advice New Zealand, and many other organisations. Jan joined a local Business Network International (BNI) group, and SheEO (an

International Women's Network). Jan also contacted Business Mentors New Zealand and got herself a business mentor, "Who was brutal – but it was a very valuable experience for me", she said.

Jan started her business in August 2021, the week New Zealand went into another major COVID lockdown. "It was a scary time", but she was convinced she had made the right decision – after all, "No job is secure. There is a massive shortage of skills in this area".

Jan was very systematic in her approach, and this has paid off big time. In less than a year Jan's business grew exponentially. Establishing her niche, she's taken on staff, and has plans to expand her business.

John Skene – Aviation History Advocate

Aircraft have always been John's passion. As a teenager he was a member of the Air Training Corps, and on leaving school he completed an engineering apprenticeship with the National Airways Corporation (NAC) in Christchurch, where he was employed. He learned to fly in Piper Cherokee and Beagle Pup aircraft with the Canterbury Aero Club where he gained his pilot's licence. "I flew for the sheer joy of it. Learning to fly also helped my appreciation of aircraft engineering".

At NAC he worked on DC3, Fokker Friendship, Vickers Viscount, and Boeing 737-200 aircraft. In later years, he worked on Boeing 737-300, ATR, and Boeing 747 aircraft under the Air New Zealand banner. As the Certifying Engineer in the Air New Zealand engine overhaul shop at Christchurch Airport, he inspected and signed off the repairs other aircraft engineers had completed for Rolls Royce

Dart and Pratt and Whitney JT8D engines for their fleet and for a growing customer base. Over time, his experience grew as the Airbus 320-200 and Boeing 777 aircraft were added to the Air New Zealand fleet. Moving to the North Island John became an Airworthiness Inspector with the Civil Aviation Authority (CAA), a role he maintained into what would traditionally be called his 'retirement years'.

In semi-retirement John set up his business 'Ardrossan Holdings Ltd' – and now, as a solo-entrepreneur, he undertakes auditing and other contract work for aircraft authorities. Over more than six decades John has accumulated a large collection of aviation books, an extensive collection of aviation memorabilia, and has good contacts with other world-wide collectors. Given his passion, research, and practical experience, he is an authority on a wide range of aircraft, their engines and the people associated with them. In this capacity he has become known as an Aviation History Advocate, whereby he assists people to research their civil and/or military aviation projects and document their personal aviation experiences and stories. Check out his website John Skene - Aviation History Advocate - Aviation Tales (aviation-tales.com)

John shares his aviation knowledge and stories with the community in his monthly radio programme called 'Aviation Past and Present' (see Aviation, Past and Present, coastaccessradio.org.nz for details). He also makes presentations to schools, clubs, and organisations on request. Currently he's in the process of publishing a collection of stories he has written about aircraft and the people connected with them.

It's been an incredible learning journey for John, "At 70 years of age, I feel like I'm only just getting started. All my experiences to date add up, and I'm looking forward to what's coming next".

Heather Knewstubb – Time Genie

Heather has a teaching and health promotion background in both the education and health sectors and pursued her interests in music and the creative arts. She enjoyed these roles, but as time passed, she became tired of the daily commute to work, wanted to spend more time with her elderly mother and was thinking about the future. What Heather wanted was a change in lifestyle. Taking on a part time job, which reduced her commute, allowed her more time to spend with her mum. It also gave her the time to develop her business idea 'Time Genie' – a personal concierge service for individuals and small businesses that she'd provide on an as needs basis.

Whilst working in her part-time role, Heather established her concierge business. She joined lots of networks to get to know people, distributed flyers, developed a website, and took on all kinds of work – it didn't matter what it was. Through referrals she was introduced to two clients who worked in education. Given her experience, this work really resonated with her, so she gave up her part-time job to put more hours into her business. Then the COVID-19 pandemic struck! Suddenly the world was in a quandary.

To focus her efforts through this trying period, Heather invested in a business coach to help her to find her niche – the client group she wanted to work with and the nature of the work she really wanted to do. Heather discovered, "I wanted to work with creative and educational clients, who are passionate and skilled in their own zone, but recognise that they can't do everything. I have the background, skills, experience, and the networks in this sector, and I work with them to understand their business and their aspirations". Knowing her niche made all the difference to how Heather marketed her business, and the nature of the work she was offering.

Time Genie was transformed and now provides "Support Services for Creative and Educational Businesses" (www.timegenie.co.nz).

"I work with a variety of like-minded people in New Zealand and Australia, who are excited about the future, and I am part of that journey. All my regular clients have got big things happening. The work is intellectually stimulating, challenging, and I'm utilising all of my skills. The great thing is, as their businesses thrive and grow, so does mine".

Karen Radford and Stephen Sexton – DRI Sleeper

Karen comes from a long line of 'hard grafters' – businesspeople, retailers, entrepreneurs.

"Growing up we learned by example that risk and hard work create opportunities and rewards".

Karen has worked in various sectors including government, retail, and not-for-profit, and has strong customer service skills. When she turned 50, Karen decided she wanted to do something for New Zealand Inc. Karen had never worked in manufacturing or export, so she joined forces with Stephen Sexton, who had extensive experience in finance, biotech, and manufacturing, both in New Zealand and overseas. They decided to, "take a bit of a risk, go into business together and at least give it a try".

They did their research and considered many businesses before deciding to buy an existing business – 'DRI Sleeper'.

"We read the prospectus, looked at the products, and thought – bedwetting alarms– products ripe for online selling, given the 'embarrassment factor' for parents and given the disintermediation that was occurring because of the internet and the ability of people to go direct to the manufacturer. Bedwetting creates trauma for families. What they need is a trusted solution. We were looking for a business that we believed in, that was solution focused rather than product focused. A business that offered flexitime that we would enjoy, as we are in this for the long haul. We examined the competition and found few alarm manufacturers were in the online space in a significant way, and most alarms were manufactured in China. It was a perfect solution and there was room for growth. After a lengthy negotiation, we agreed a price".

It took Karen and Stephen years to grow and develop the business and increase brand awareness. "Our products are designed and manufactured in Christchurch, and we distribute them to wholesalers, hospitals, and to individuals and families in New Zealand and overseas. Using smart technology, everything can be purchased directly from us online via www.dri-sleeper.com and we also sell our products through Amazon".

Karen said, they had a lot of lean years, but it was worth the effort.

"We set new milestones every few months and have a loyal support team and a wide network of contractors we can call upon. Our business isn't constricted geographically, but we do have to comply with New Zealand and international trade agreements to export our goods to Europe, the United States, the United Kingdom, Canada, and Asia. Each country has its own compliance requirements and regulations, and this process can be onerous for a small business".

Hitting new highs, this business continues to be very rewarding for Karen and Stephen. "As we provide something valuable and worthwhile for others, and are comfortable in the digital world, the options for our business are limitless. The nature of this business also enables us to maintain a flexible and interesting lifestyle into our retirement years".

Cathy Sheppard – BSI People Skills

Passionate about learning, Cathy home schooled her children. With more than 20 years' work experience in early childhood and secondary schools, she also provided professional development solutions for people working in these environments. In mid-life, she became disenchanted when she realised that there was virtually nothing in the job market that gave her the opportunity to use her skills. "I wanted to offer my own development programmes, based on good design, to empower people and transform workplace and educational spaces. This meant going into business and my sister encouraged me to go for it".

With three children at home, Cathy initially started her business on a part-time basis, but things moved too slowly. "I wanted to offer totally tailored solutions to address specific issues and I knew I needed to collaborate with others to do this. I made the leap, let go of my part-time job and went into my business full-time with no clients. Although I didn't have a business background, I had a strong vision that I believed in. Everything I do is about people and is purpose based. I want them to get up every morning and feel empowered".

It was a steep learning curve, but one Cathy was prepared to take. Intrinsically driven, she fully understood her strengths, skills, and experience, and was prepared to take the risk. She leveraged her existing network of contacts, developed relationships with a diverse range of individuals and organisations in Aotearoa and offshore, and developed an online presence (www.bsipeopleskills.co.nz).

"Using a consultative model, and drawing on our expertise, we work in partnership with teams to understand the culture of the organisation, find out what's going on, and see how we can make the biggest difference".

In collaboration with other professionals, the team at BSI have facilitated coaching sessions and workshops in New Zealand, Bangladesh, Malaysia, Nepal, and Bali and offer online programmes. In a nutshell, "BSI works on a global scale with businesses who truly value their people", say Cathy.

Phil Byrne – Eco Shifter

An engineer by trade, Phil had worked with aviation companies all his life. At 55 years of age, he felt it was the time to do something different and enjoy a more balanced lifestyle. Phil and his partner Kay moved to the Kapiti Coast and as they settled into their new home, they mulled over their ideas to start a business. The 'aha' moment came when a local retailer delivered their new fridge. "I watched as the delivery vehicle reversed into our driveway puffing great clouds of smoke. I helped the guy unload our new fridge and then watched as the vehicle drove away in another great plume of smoke, leaving behind a big puddle of oil in our driveway". It wasn't the first time he had witnessed this scenario.

Phil had always been concerned about the environment and wanted to do what he could to reduce the carbon footprint. A regular at the gym he was physically fit and healthy, highly self-motivated, liked people and was willing to help them. He knew he could offer a quality eco-friendly delivery service, and he could pick up and make deliveries at a time that suited the customer, rather than the time that worked for the supplier. In a nutshell, his vision was to establish, 'a fast, reliable, cost-effective, environmentally friendly pick-up and delivery service'.

After researching his business idea, 'Eco Shifter' was formed. Within a few short months his first fully electric delivery vehicle was providing a 24-hour service, seven days a week for customers across the Wellington, Kapiti and Horowhenua regions. He developed a website (www.ecoshifter.nz). Within a short period of time the business grew to the extent Phil employed staff and purchased additional vehicles. Eco Shifter clearly provides a much-needed service for the community as Phil often gets repeat business from his customers which, he says, "is very satisfying".

Phil made a successful mid-life transition and loves working in his business. "The nature of the work keeps me fit and healthy; I have the freedom to work hours that work for me and my customers; I get to help people every day offering an efficient environmentally friendly service; I have the flexibility to undertake more voluntary work; and I'm having fun".

Phil's venture has been so successful he's expanding his business in other locations and is now offering Franchise options. If you are interested – get in touch.

Raewynne Graf – Ātahu Hosted Accommodation
Fully Self-contained suite and Studio

Raewynne has extensive project management experience on both sides of the Tasman. While working in Australia for nine years, she rented out her two properties in New Zealand, and with the income generated on both sides of the Tasman, she paid off the mortgage and built up her assets. In her mid-60's she returned home, with no plans to retire. Intending to start a new venture, she sold off one of her homes, and was going to build apartments on the section. After having architectural plans drawn up of two apartments and a new home, she still deliberated if this was the best way to develop her property. After sharing a wine with a couple friends, she went back to the drawing board and viewed the existing cottage on the property in Titahi Bay and changed her mind. "I really liked this home on the seafront", and after further reflection and business research she decided to keep it and develop it into a rental property.

"I knew I could enjoy a flexible relaxed lifestyle and run a business from home. I had a clear vision of what I wanted, and I have strong project management skills. I did my research and made plans to move the cottage forward on the section nearer the road, leaving room to build a fully Self-contained suite, and a Studio as part of my new home, which would create a stream of income. I wanted higher end, quality hosted accommodation, all built independently, with the flexibility to subdivide the sections in the future".

Raewynne, as an independent woman, found the building project a challenge, especially during the worst of the COVID pandemic. Family members were busy getting on with their own lives, but luckily close friends kept in touch and supported her through many difficult phases of the build. They were always there to cheer her on and help celebrate her successes. A great lover of gardens, Raewynne carefully planned the landscaping, and enjoyed planting out the property herself. Regrettably, following a couple of major storms, some areas of the section had to be re-planted. Although disheartening, it wasn't an insurmountable setback.

With a big investment in the planning stage, the restrictions around the pandemic, compounded by a shortage of reliable, skilled tradespeople, every aspect of the building project took a lot longer than she anticipated. But Raewynne never lost faith.

"What has kept me going was my vision. I kept looking at my plans and reminded myself why I was doing this. I called my property Ātahu – it means 'charm or spell'".

Situated 21 kilometres from Wellington, **and two** minutes from the beach, Raewynne's Self-contained suite, and a Studio, both with sea views, are now available to guests. Bookings can be made directly with Raewynne by email (matatiro@yahoo.co.nz/ raewynne@atahu.nz, or online https://atahu.nz).

Angela Robertson – Maximising Potential

I always loved learning. For more than 30-years I enjoyed a successful career supporting individuals, organisations, and communities to identify, develop and capitalise on their talent. I developed frameworks; researched and developed programmes and resources and facilitated workshops and conferences. It was a privilege. On reaching middle-essence, I was tired of the 1,000 kilometre a week commute to work that I'd been doing for decades. It was time to recharge my batteries and have the freedom and the flexibility to expand and leverage my skills and experience to maximise potential in the wider community.

Taking a big step, I resigned from my role. People asked "what will you do" – but I knew infinite possibilities and opportunities were out there for me. I just needed to find them. A friend suggested I join forces with others and start a community network for people like myself who wanted to start a business or who had started a business in later life. We did. The Kapiti/Horowhenua Entrepreneurs @ 50+ Network, now in its fourth year, provides reciprocal encouragement and practical support for the members to achieve their aspirations and goals, without the need for expensive membership fees.

Colleagues I worked with in the past offered me research, resource development projects, speaking engagements, and one-on-one coaching contracts - assignments I enjoy, appreciate and am good at. I love the variety of work in this space, and it keeps me connected with the workplace. I developed a website, which was a completely new experience for me (www.angelarobertson.nz).

Meanwhile, I began writing cameo short stories about real people, living in Aotearoa, who, like me are in the second half of life. The people I wrote about believe life is a continuous adventure. We can change gears and direction and expand our horizons at any age if we want to. These stories morphed into the four collections of stories in the *'Older and Bolder'* series of books (Amazon.com: Angela Robertson: Books, Biography, Blog, Audiobooks, Kindle). This led to a host of speaking engagements around the country and requests to assist people with their memoirs. In this capacity, I work one-on-one with private clients and facilitate community workshops to help others document their own stories, family histories and/or spiritual journeys. In hindsight, there was an impulse and a strong desire to create living legacies, something that connects communities of people to future generations. It's been a privilege.

Oliver Wendall Holmes once said,

"Every calling is great when greatly pursued".

Wise words I've taken to heart. I maximise potential, regardless of age and stage, which includes my own. As an author, inspirational speaker, facilitator, and coach I'm passionate about my work, and channel my energy into activities that matter and the people who truly want to flourish. As the saying goes, 'do what you love, and the money will follow'.

By the time most of us reach 'Middlescence', we want to leverage the wealth of knowledge, skills, and experience we've accrued, and continue to be productive, but not necessarily in the same way, or working for someone else. We begin to question the status quo, and wonder 'what's next'. While continuing to find paid work can be a challenge, it can be liberating to acknowledge you no longer need to fit into the 'employee' box with any specific organisation. Or you may no longer need or want to earn a big salary at the expense of an enjoyable, balanced, and rewarding lifestyle. The opportunity to follow a passion, explore new opportunities, craft new ways of working with different people, make our own decisions, eliminate unnecessary lengthy commutes, and at the same time reconnect and a make a difference in the community can be enticing.

And it's achievable.

6 Identified a Gap/Opportunity in the Marketplace

Identifying a gap in the marketplace and being prepared to seize the opportunity to fill it is a strong foundation for a business. Often entrepreneurs come up with an idea for a business when they themselves have either become frustrated with the lack of a particular product or service, or they have identified a solution to a problem and know that they can do something about it. Taking the time to understand your market, and the challenges potential customers can face can be a great source of inspiration and can help you to position your product and/or service to bridge the gap.

Let's hear from eight entrepreneurs who did just that – sometimes more than once!

Molly Burke – Second Act Services

In her early 60's Molly made a major life change when, sight unseen, she moved from her home in San Francisco to New Zealand with her kiwi partner. In three short years, she re-established her existing coaching business in the southern hemisphere and pursued her artistic and cultural interests in the Horowhenua. Then along came COVID – the trigger. The global pandemic caused severe social and economic disruption. Millions died, millions more became seriously ill, and most, but not all of them were in the older age group. Lifestyles changed on a global scale, as we became more aware of our own mortality. In business, the word 'pivot' was on the tip of everyone's tongue. To survive the global recession, businesses had to 'pivot' – by taking a hard look at their products, services, and practices, and changing their approach to meet customer demand and to remain viable.

Like many, Molly, in her mid-60's, considered the future. The pandemic hit her coaching business hard, and in later life, she too wanted to pivot. She wanted to transition into something else, have a better, more flexible lifestyle, contribute in some way, and make the most of her energy levels, her skills, and her time. She had no intention of retiring.

Molly recognised that others were in this same situation. She considered the disabled and marginalised members of the community. She also considered athletes, dancers, musicians, artists, and tradespeople, who couldn't pursue the careers they'd previously enjoyed because their bodies couldn't take it any longer. For these individuals, and many more like them, it was time to 'pivot' - change direction. This was Molly's driver – her **WHY**.

Molly applied the 'pivot' principle to her own business and her personal life. Her new coaching business, 'Second Act Services' – helps people in their 40's, 50's, and 60's, to pivot - to refocus and transition into something else that suits them better – this is her **WHAT**.

HOW did she do this? "As soon as I got this idea, I took action to make this business happen. I immediately updated my website (COVID-19 | Second Act Services/career change (mollyburke.net) and, let everyone know that they were not alone during the lockdowns. Curious to know what was out there, I realised, I already had a professional toolkit, that I used in my coaching business and my professional life. My previous business had been referral driven – I wanted to niche down. Now I reapply my skills and experience to this demographic in the community. I only accept projects that I am passionate about in this target market".

Pivoting herself, Molly and her partner sold their home in the Horowhenua and moved into their 'forever' home in Whanganui. "I saw this as an adventure. It's the opportunity to live a bohemian lifestyle in later life, focus my energy on what's important, meet new people, apply my skills, work fewer hours, and still have time to pursue my passions".

Denise Carnihan - Kailani Pearl Swim

Yes, that's right, we are re-visiting Denise Carnihan. When COVID struck, her African tour business, literally came to a grinding halt with the first lockdown. She had multiple African tours fully booked two years ahead – but the borders were closed. The international travel we'd previously enjoyed, ceased to exist. In the doldrums, she lived in hope that the airlines and the tours would start up again, but no one knew when. This was the trigger to dabble in other travel ventures on the domestic market and in Rarotonga. Fortunately, Denise, now in her 60's, kept her networks open, and people, eager to travel, booked trips. But the pandemic prevailed, it was a tumultuous time, full of uncertainly and disappointment. When the traffic light system was introduced, the trips had to be cancelled.

Meanwhile as summer approached, Denise searched for her swimming togs. They were a pair she'd designed and made herself in attractive fabric, as there was nothing appealing about the ill-fitting, great grandma type togs that were on offer for older women (55–70-year-olds) in the shops. Frustrated, that her home-made togs couldn't be found when she needed them Denise identified a gap in the market, "If I had a problem, then other women did too", she said. This was her **WHY**.

Denise is never short of ideas and is quick to act on them. "I had lots of ideas for attractive togs, that fit well, are easy to get in and out of, made with beautiful fabrics for women in my age range". She joined a sewing group on Facebook, did her research, and identified the pain points for women in this market – her **WHAT**.

Rather than make the togs herself, she engaged a graduate to design a range of mix and match Tankini top and pant togs. "Subsequently a portfolio of 10 designs were developed, all with a nice shape, good support, with a choice of boy-leg and other shaped pants, easy wear, with zips as a feature, and matching accessories, thus addressing all the annoying pain points".

In the background, Denise created an avatar of the person she was making these togs for and created a brand. She researched and sourced gorgeous eco-ethical active wear fabrics, made in Italy from recycled ocean waste (e.g., fish nets and plastic bottles), that has been completely regenerated eliminating all the nasty stuff. Denise learned there was only one company in the world that could make it with licensed agents, but the products were too expensive to make in New Zealand. Undeterred Denise approached a family business in Bali that had the appropriate license. She selected the print designs and hired the family business to make samples from the sketches provided. When the international borders opened Denise went to Bali for the fitting, as all the samples were made in her own size to make sure they had it right. Videos were taken on site, to be used for promotional purposes on her new website (www.kailanipearl.com). The Kailani Pearl swimwear range was launched in September 2022 and marketed to her existing clients and networks.

It's amazing what you can achieve when you put your time and energy into a project you feel strongly about and are prepared to learn on the run as Denise did. The whole process took Denise five-months from whoa to go. What's more, this business is complementary with her travel business.

Incidentally, Kailani is Hawaiian for 'sea and sky', and this is her granddaughter Mia's middle name. Naturally, Denise's husband Chris is incredibly supportive and proud of his wife's achievements.

Anne Russell and Rosemary Emery – Off the Page

Anne, a trained primary school teacher, has extensive experience in special education. She consults in her own business (Offbeat Education) and has developed three special education resource books for teachers. Rosemary, a special education teacher and speech language therapist, works with children and adults with all kinds of disabilities. These two women have decades of practical experience in their field. They fully understand the issues and have an affinity for the children and adults involved. In their 50's, the inspiration for 'Off the Page' came to them from a persistent call from schools for age-appropriate books for young adults with low reading levels. "Unfortunately, there were no resources available - children's books and picture books for infants did not appeal to young adults" – this was the trigger.

Anne and Rosemary believe it's important that students are seen as teenagers and young people first, and their reading ability second – not the other way around. They needed teaching resources for parents and teachers working with teenagers and young adults with special needs or reading difficulties. These had to be resources that, "Open the Mind to the World of Words by reaching out to young adults and providing them with a range of topics that motivated and inspired them to read", – their very strong **WHY**.

Although working in their substantive roles, these women undertook global research to see what was 'out there'. They found lots of resources, but none were suitable for the age range and interest levels, and with this their concept was born. "We will research, design and develop resources in a form that captures the imagination of young adults, as well as developing their reading and comprehension abilities". Anne and Rosemary had discovered their **WHAT**.

Collaborating on the project, Anne and Rosemary researched in depth, the literacy stages and developed a framework for three emergent reading levels, each with an increasing level of difficulty. They worked hard to develop eBooks that engage reluctant and low ability readers, as well as resources for teachers and parents to encourage reading and word awareness. With the support of Business Mentors, they developed a business plan, a Mission Statement, a brand, and a website (www.offthepage.co.nz), where their extensive range of quality books are sold online – this is **HOW** Anne and Rosemary went about developing their business. Over time, they have created dozens of titles on a wide range of topics that appeal to teenagers and young adults, with realistic photos that are motivating and age appropriate, and ultimately help their readers to develop their skills and a love of reading.

Furthermore, their business, which is meeting the needs of these young people, is entirely self-funded. This is an amazing accomplishment considering they both have 'day jobs', and families of their own.

Tom Rodden - Peak Coaching

Tom had been a school principal for more than 30 years. It was a stressful job with responsibility for 50+ staff, 500 kids, some of whom had special education needs, and parents who had high expectations.

Tom said, "By this stage, some of my colleagues had died, and others had various illnesses. It was a wakeup call - I thought this could be me! I knew I had 15-20 productive years ahead of me and wanted to do something else".

Tom changed direction when he purchased Raumati Sands - an apartment business. He successfully made the transition and over the next nine years increased revenue and efficiency. "When I employed a manager I thought - where to from here"? Sharing his success Tom became a business coach and advisor and assisted others grappling with running a business and cashflow. "When it came time for me to sell Raumati Sands and relocate to Taranaki, I was confronted with more questions than answers. I had to navigate my way through a myriad of challenges and pitfalls to make a successful exit". Realising that others in business must face the same dilemma, Tom also appreciated the fact that no one needed this level of stress when exiting their business. His personal experience and lessons learned along the way provided him with his **WHY**.

Identifying a gap in the market, and therefore an opportunity, he started a new business. As 'Head Exitologist', he assists people to prepare to exit their business. As part of his service, Tom helps people explore ways of adding value by making their business attractive to buyers, and ensure they have an effective and timely handover to the new owners.

Relocating to Taranaki, Tom immediately set to work turning his ideas into a reality. He joined lots of networks to intentionally build strong face-to-face and online relationships within the wider community. Tom developed a range of coaching and mentoring programmes to help individuals grow the value of their business and position it for sale, and promoted them on his new website Peak Coaching | How prepared is your business for sale? Utilising his skills, he wrote an e.Book, several articles for newspapers and magazines, and gave seminars to interested groups such as the Chamber of Commerce. In effect, Tom established a niche – everyone needs to exit their business at some stage, so why leave this to chance?

Liz Koh – Enrich Retirement

Liz established a very successful financial planning company called Moneymax. For more than 20 years she provided personalised financial planning and common-sense advice to thousands of people, and as a result her business flourished. In her early 60's she decided to change direction, step away from Moneymax, and focus on her long-term dream – to set up a website where people could access all the tools and information, they need to plan their own retirement.

In the years leading up to this decision, Liz was inundated with questions from people who were about to retire. "They had no idea how to start planning the most important stage of their lives, or where to go to get the information and resources that were available to them". Liz wanted to share her own knowledge, skills, and experience, along with information, tools and learning resources provided by experts in this field, with a much bigger audience. Her mission for 'Enrich Retirement' is to provide a global online service to empower individuals to live their retirement to the max.

Although Liz had the idea for her online business in her mind for a long time, she developed her ideas over a three-year period. She was also careful to plan how she would let go of Moneymax, transition into her new business, and at the same time meet her voluntary commitments in the community, which are very important to her. Reflecting on her transferrable skills, Liz invested in her own development, and made the decision to hire the best to develop a quality website Enrich Retirement - Retirement Education, Revolutionised the platform for her online business. Technically savvy, she learned how to develop webinars. She also bought a flash new camera and learned how to use that too. Liz developed a network of affiliates and choosing her distribution channels wisely, she developed a three-year plan to build the reputation of the business and achieve her marketing goals.

Liz said, "I'm excited about doing something people really need and want. Enrich Retirement has so much potential. People are genuinely interested, and the services provided really do fill the gap. It always takes longer than we think to start a business and develop it, but quality is everything, and I know I add value".

Ken and Judith Shilling – Tisco and Link Technology

There are always exceptions. Ken and Judith Shilling are amongst them, so it helps to provide a snapshot of their background. On leaving school, Judith worked alongside tradesmen in a garage where she gained strong business and administrative skills. Aged 15, Ken began a plumbing apprenticeship under the guidance of this father, who came out of retirement to train him. Ken's dad taught him everything he knew about the technical aspects of the trade, as well as the administrative side of the family business (e.g., marketing, quotes for services, and invoicing). At 21 years of age after completing his 12,000 hours apprenticeship and examinations, Ken was a fully qualified 'Craftsman' in his trade. When Ken married Judith, he inherited 'Shilling Plumbing' the family business in Nelson. Working as a team, Ken undertook all the plumbing work, Judith managed the administration and the business flourished. By the time Ken was 24, he employed three plumbers to help him provide quality plumbing services to his customers.

In his late 20's, in response to a medical issue, Ken changed direction. For the next 16 years, he enjoyed a successful career in the insurance industry. Exposed to a completely different industry, he learned a lot in the corporate environment. As a National Marketing Manager for an insurance company Ken was part of a merger team for the company's rural services. The merger exposed Ken to the Head of Marketing at Harvard, and a Logistics change manager from Australia who passed on skills available only to a few. But Ken disliked the toxic environment of the corporate world and elected to accept the offer of redundancy and the opportunity to branch out on his own again.

Excited about his next step, Ken spent two weeks writing a business plan on the basis, 'if you don't know where you are going anywhere will do'! Starting as a sole trader, he offered plumbing services and together with Judith who was then working in real estate, they targeted identified markets. Later they formed 'Guildcraft Projects with Trades' in Wellington, a franchise operation in multiple trades for highly skilled craftsmen, offering superior customer service. As the franchisor, Ken provided mentoring, training with certification and endorsements, support for the franchisees, and with a bigger group was able to offer them cost efficiencies for tools and supplies. Judith provided administrative support for the organisation. It was a very successful business model. Over time, many of the franchisees wanted to break away from the larger group to form their own independent businesses, so Ken and Judith made the decision to put Guildcraft Projects with Trades into liquidation.

Meanwhile the wave of rapid technological change gained momentum in New Zealand. Unlike many, Judith, and Ken, (who was then in his mid-50's), embraced the technological revolution. Recognising an opportunity, they changed direction, and became early adopters in their next business venture. Encouraged by their son's interest in electronics, they bought 'Tisco NZ Ltd.', in 2002 as a going concern. The domestic and corporate market for the installation and repair of electronic appliances was, and still is, huge. Now Tisco is known as *the most trusted name in electronics for over 60 years.'* For more details check out this website www.tisco.net.nz

While a typical entrepreneur might start one business venture and stick with it, a serial entrepreneur often starts and runs more than one business (or multiple businesses) simultaneously, or successively, one after another. With Ken's entrepreneurial spirit, he and Judith have owned and operated several businesses over the years, as his visionary business ideas and interest in technological solutions continued to evolve. After 40 years in the service industry, using innovative software solutions the couple identified another opportunity in the marketplace. Their new business, called 'Link Technology', helps importers, retailers, and repairers to provide warranty, repair, and installation services to the customer through a diversified service network. Using the latest technology – a centralized workflow system, the whole process is fully automated and is managed by Ken and Judith, from their home. Manufacturers, importers, inventory and warehouses, retailers, installers, repairers, and insurance companies interact on a central platform. The contracted-out call centre facility assists customers with their enquiries and creates jobs for a network of installer/repairers and matches local service providers with the appropriate credentials directly with the customer. The web store provides access to goods and service 24/7, and the warehouses dispatch inventory on request.

The cloud-based application provides centralised, transparent, visibility for everyone involved, in every step of the service delivery process. Ultimately this system connects everyone in the service chain, drives superior quality service delivery, and minimises the cost of administration and labour. Ken said, "It pays to hire a good accountant and lawyer and an excellent software developer who understands your vision and requirements and delivers the best service". To learn more, check out this website www.linktechnology.net

Around 2010, in response to requests from their customers, the Shilling's Link Technology business expanded to Australia using the same software and processes. They trained a local master agent to act, and the venture was very successful. Seven years later, the master agent like Guildcraft franchisees, determined they now had enough knowledge to go alone with the existing customer base. The business was shut down and the legal association with the master agent was terminated.

Undeterred, aged 69, Ken opened a new business in Melbourne called Chain.Net Propriety. An Australian Director was appointed to run the operation and three non-exclusive master agents were engaged and trained. Despite the impact of the global pandemic, which struck hard just as the business was just getting off the ground, Chain.Net Propriety Ltd., has weathered the storm and is now on course to be successful.

Judith and Ken have worked exceptionally well together as a team for 53 years. It's fascinating to gain insight into the story behind their success and see how their ideas came to fruition. With complementary skills and experience, clearly defined roles, a passion for learning, efficiency, and quality service provision, they've taken risks, moved with the times, and tapped into the people with the appropriate knowledge and expertise to bring their business ideas to life.

It's apparent that business ideas can come from anywhere and there are occasions when individuals stumble across an opportunity and take steps to bridge the gap. The experience and perspective of the entrepreneurs that feature in this chapter, helped them identify an unmet need and prompted them to do something about it.

The key was knowing their strengths, tapping into their existing skills and experience, doing the market research, understanding the landscape, taking calculated risks, and maximising the use of technology to deliver products and services. It's also evident that businesses evolve through a process of managed trial and error.

Your turn

There are innumerable ways of resolving problems and frustrations once they've been identified.   If you'd like to give it a try, start by identifying a range of potential issues and brainstorm possible solutions. Ask,

- What have other people tried to do in this area?
- What has worked and what hasn't - and why?
- What positive changes can I make to fulfil an unmet need?

When considering the various issues, frustrations and/or opportunities, flesh out a range of different scenarios. Anticipate the potential impact of cultural, economic, social, environmental, and technological change on your community, industry, sector, or lifestyle and ask 'what if' questions to see where these ideas lead.

7 Mindset

Regardless of the circumstances, transitions are never easy. Whenever we take up a new pursuit, whether it's a sport, hobby, health regime, project, or occupation, it requires significant effort, persistence, and momentum to make things happen to achieve our goals to maintain momentum, and there is always a learning curve. Entrepreneurs generally tend to have a 'learn-as-you-go spirit'. This obviously varies to a greater or lesser degree depending on the nature and scale of the task, the situation and conditions, and access to the required funds. It also depends on the mindset, knowledge, skills, and experience of the people concerned, as well as the financial and other support provided. Often, we anticipate some of the challenges. We know there will be an element of risk, trials and tribulations, and hurdles to overcome on this journey. There will be people to meet, new skills to learn, investments to be made, and decisions to make.

Sometimes these challenges are negligible, while others may be huge and take us by surprise - for example the global COVID pandemic! Regardless, successful entrepreneurs, bounce back from setbacks, disappointments, and sometimes from major crises, and we can all learn from the experience.

Everyone is unique and if we want to stand out from the crowd it's important to know and embrace our own uniqueness – our unique talents and abilities. At 50+, we have already amassed half a lifetime of knowledge, skills, and experience and often seek the chance to do something we want to do, rather than what anyone else wants us to do. If we take an inventory of our strengths, know how best to use them, and consciously decide to intentionally leverage them, it's more likely that we will be successful. (Use this link to **complete the Gallup Clifton Strengthsfinder Top 5 Strengths online assessment** (http://gallupstrengthscenter.com/ - I also recommend a book 'Flourish' by Martin Seligman).

It's impossible to stretch yourself, change gears and direction, to have or be more, if you don't step outside your comfort zone. We are all comfortable with what is familiar to us, but it isn't enough when we want to achieve more in life. Importantly, we need to recognise when we don't have the requisite skills, and either be prepared to develop them or be willing to tap into the strengths and expertise others can provide.

We'll examine some of these factors in the pages to come. But first let's consider the underlying factor – mindset! We all have a set of beliefs that influence how we: -

- Think, question, learn and make sense of the world,
- Feel,
- Identify, interpret, and respond to opportunities and challenges,
- Communicate with ourselves, about ourselves, and about others,
- Interact with others,
- Make choices.

We've established that there needs to be a burning desire and a strong belief in your **WHY** and the self-confidence and the motivation to work towards your **WHAT,** when starting a business. This usually means programming yourself for success by: -

- Moving out of familiar routines where we feel safe and in control,
- Committing to our goal,
- Expecting to be uncomfortable with the unfamiliar,
- Taking small steps to overcome our fears - we all have them,
- Starting small, debt free if possible, and keeping the costs low. Starting a business doesn't always require a big budget but there will be set-up, and operating costs,
- Asking for help e.g., mentoring, support, advice, and hiring contractors to undertake work you either don't enjoy, or are not good at, to free up the time you can spend on other tasks.
- Acquiring new skills e.g., getting to grips with, and keeping up to date with the constant changes in technology, appreciating it's never too late to learn,
- Taking calculated risks,
- Anticipating and dealing with difficulties and problems as they arise,
- Managing our self-talk - the internal chatterbox that loves to criticise what we do, and how we do it, and provides us with excuses,
- Avoiding the naysayers - these people who don't want us to change gears, who want the status quo,
- Learning from our mistakes - we all make them,
- Recognising and accepting that it takes time to establish a business, and gain momentum in the marketplace, and
- Appreciating that business ideas evolve over time. Some people pursue ideas, and it all works out just as they had planned. Other times, ideas evolve, and individuals change direction.

It seems like a big list – but it's doable, and necessary, depending on your mindset, otherwise we'll give up when the going gets tough. Every one of the entrepreneurs who feature in this book took these steps. Regardless of the trigger, they all have a strong belief in their **WHY** and the mindset, motivation, and determination to work towards achieving their **WHAT**. In effect, they all made a commitment to move out of their comfort zone and a willingness to deal with whatever challenges they may face.

Andrew Burn commented, "Without realising it, we sometimes build our own prison, and then we find it hard to get out of it. Of course, it's scary, but it's also exciting going into the unknown, and I've never looked back".

Cathy Sheppard made a leap of faith and went into her business full-time with no clients.

Once Paul Streekstra had decided to go into business for himself, he realised, "The options were limitless".

And reflecting on her learning journey Kareen Holland said, "I'm proud that I started from zero in my 50's as a single mum. I'm now the sole owner of a manufacturing, retail, and wholesale business, and offer a range of beauty treatments. It's such an achievement".

Denise, a serial entrepreneur who comes up with multiple ideas for business opportunities asks herself, "What's the worst that can happen?" Denise is also prepared to let an idea, or business go when she wants to move on to something more interesting, or more viable.

Some ideas work and others don't. It helps to keep things in perspective. And, as you are in the driver's seat, it's over to you whether you stay in any particular business for the long haul or not.

Here are six common fears all budding entrepreneurs learn to deal with, regardless of their age and stage: -

1. Believing in yourself, your product and/or your service,
2. Making the commitment,
3. Getting started – or not knowing where to start,
4. Putting your work out there,
5. Not attracting customers, and
6. Failure. Maybe the idea doesn't work out.

With the right attitude to life, we can address and deal with most of these fears, and the hurdles that come our way. **It's a learning curve. If others can do it, so can you.** We don't necessarily have to have all the answers before we start but we do need to be optimistic, open to developing new skills, prepared to learn from our experience, manage the way we communicate with ourselves (our self-talk), and with others, and make conscious choices.

In the start-up phase, when running a business, and as the business evolves, we all experience rough patches of one kind or another. When faced with challenges it's so important to remain optimistic about your business and your future. If you are optimistic, you'll learn from your experience, be more likely to seek help, and be motivated to take whatever action is required to achieve what you want e.g., identify new opportunities, seek creative ways to expand, to change or add new products or services, and keep moving towards success.

In the next chapter we'll examine some of the common challenges encountered by the entrepreneurs who feature in this book.

8 Common Challenges, Lessons Learned, Tips and Techniques, and Useful Websites

Regardless of your skills and wealth of previous experience, it's a challenge to start and run your own business. Yes, we all know there will be hurdles along the way, some are just minor irritations and others may seem huge, - but with an open mind, the right attitude, and a great support network of like-minded people, nothing is insurmountable. Transitions for most people, are never easy – whether good or bad, they bring a degree of anxiety and uncertainty. There is no one path to follow. Although we may not realise it at the time, it's usually the challenges we encounter in life that stretch us and make life much more interesting.

In this chapter we'll explore the most common problems shared by entrepreneurs who started their business @ 50+. In response to some of these challenges tips are offered that may be useful for those of you who have recently started or are planning to start a business.

Funding a business

Start-up costs for new businesses vary, whatever your age and stage in life. In later life, many of us, but not all, are financially stable, own property, and savings may have been accrued. In Marie Hannan's case, she tapped into her superannuation to set up her business the Nepal New Zealand Connection. People in the second half of life don't necessarily want to invest thousands of dollars in a new venture, expensive equipment, additional qualifications, lavish marketing campaigns, or get into debt. But there are exceptions.

Similarly, successful later life entrepreneurs, may not want to work fulltime in the business or have profit only motives. While generating a sustainable income they often want to utilise their skills and experience to create or contribute something meaningful to the community and make a real difference e.g., make a social or environmental impact.

It's strongly recommended that you seek expert financial advice before taking the plunge. As personal circumstances, aspirations and the nature and scope of business ideas differ, specific detail on financing a business venture is not covered here, but a good starting point is to consider these key questions, and note your responses: -

1. What will it take and how will I fund the launch of my new venture? (Consider savings, superannuation, and grants. If I get a loan, how will I pay this back? Find out how others have raised the funds and structured their business to do the kind of things you are considering).
2. What income will I generate and where will this come from?
3. How will I fund my transition? (Unless you are lucky enough to start your business with regular clients, it's hard to predict your cash flow. You'll need a buffer to cover your expenses while you are researching and developing your resources, website etc., building a clientele, and generating a reliable source of income. This may take several months, or even years).

Reflecting on your responses to these questions, ask yourself if you are financially ready to make a change. If the answer is yes, you'll need a budget that includes the details of your start-up costs (including research and development, legal costs etc.), and your operating costs, including your salary. Also add details of your expected revenue.

Think about both the short and the long-term. Consider whether you want to stay small (e.g., operating as a micropreneur with less than five employees), or are looking to run a big operation. Do you need premises, or is it a home-based business you can operate from anywhere?

Having a regular job and starting/running a business

Some individuals make the choice of starting a business in addition to their regular employment. This strategy, popularly known as a 'side hustle', has obvious benefits. For example: -

- If you can invest the time, you may be able to create an additional stream of income while maintaining your regular income from your current job.
- While you are building your business you'll have ongoing relationships with your colleagues in the workplace, and can retain your relationships with clients in the sector you are working in.
- You may also have access to and take advantage of relevant training opportunities in your substantive role.

On the flip side:

- It takes time and energy to plan and develop your business, especially if it is in a different industry to the one you are currently working in.

- You may need to learn and apply new skills to develop your products and services and learn how to set up and manage your business, which takes time and effort.
- It's highly likely you'll still want to have time to meet and enjoy your family commitments and participate in social activities.

Anne and Rosemary enjoy their work with the education sector. They also enjoy their business - leveraging their expertise to create quality ebooks for reluctant and low ability readers, and supplementary resources for teachers and parents. Importantly, while juggling their day jobs and their business, they want to enjoy a balanced family lifestyle. Assessing their strengths and weaknesses, and to make the best use of their time, they focus their energy on what they enjoy and are good at – creating educational products. Once established, they wisely sought dedicated expertise to help them to develop their business and market their products – a necessary time-consuming activity. As a result, they've been able to free up the time they had previously spent on this activity themselves.

Jan started developing her cyber security business while she was in her substantive role, where she was doing similar work for larger organisations. She developed her website, designed, and implemented her processes, developed her report templates, and automated everything she could by investing in online tools upfront. She was also transparent in her approach, and openly advised her boss and her networks that she was going into business. Meanwhile, in her personal life she assessed her commitments and paid off her mortgage. This meant she could launch her business debt-free and hit the ground running when she resigned from her job and let go of her regular pay cheque.

Andrew said, "Letting go of my 30-year regular job, and the income it provided was daunting". It was his biggest challenge, but he needed to spend time developing his business, and that meant leaving his place of employment. The fear about this was worse than the reality. He's never looked back.

John made a conscious decision to set up his business before leaving his role with Civil Aviation. Well known in the industry, he now undertakes contracts as and when required. Elements of John's business have evolved since he gave up his job as he now has the time to develop his ideas, learn new skills and develop additional products and services.

Molly's biggest challenge was letting go of her previous business interests in entertainment. "This was a huge, but necessary decision that had to be made. I had to free up my time to focus my attention on my niche market. After so many years I miss it, but I had to pivot. It was the right decision".

Heather started small with her business idea, while she was still employed on a part-time basis. Gradually, her business evolved when she found her niche – her target market and the nature of the work she wanted to do. This was a game changer. With regular clients and increasing levels of confidence, Heather let go of her part-time job and moved into her business full-time.

If you are employed on either a part-time or fulltime basis and are serious about starting a business while you are still in your day job, you will need to manage your time and your energy. Apart from a very strong **WHY**, in a nutshell you'll need: -

- A Business Plan – which includes your target market, clear goals on what you want to achieve, how you will achieve them, a description of what success will look like, and the budget to achieve them. Your Business Plan is the blueprint for success. Taking this step pushes you to organise your thoughts, assess your strengths, weaknesses, opportunities, and threats, and answer important questions.

- Time to develop your products and services, (developing something customers want, at a price they can afford), and the tools to manage your business, including the appropriate technology.
- To be willing to work in small sprints.

You'll recall, Ken Shilling spent two weeks writing his Business Plan. As he wisely said, "It's an essential document. If you don't know where you are going, anywhere will do".

If you are looking for tips on how to write a Business Plan, check out this website **How to write a business plan — business.govt.nz**

It also helps if you team up with others to share ideas and the tasks involved and surround yourself with a great network of support.

Multitasking While Developing and Growing your Business

Entrepreneurs build their businesses from scratch. Often, they don't know where to start and may not have a clear plan of what their business is. In this case, it pays to: -

- Start small.
- Be prepared to try out different ideas, experiment.
- Find out what you like, and what you'd like to do more of.
- Learn what works, and what doesn't (e.g., what people want or need, and what generates income).

Then develop your business.

Planning and prioritising what needs to be done to structure a business and get it off the ground is a learning curve. Determining, developing, and marketing compatible products and services, and the target audience for these takes time. While low budget business ideas may not require much capital, some businesses require a significant investment to get up and running. Regardless, there will be expenses and you'll need to think about cash flow.

If manufacturing, importing and/or exporting, check the essential compliance approvals with the appropriate authorities. Note that global distribution may require compliance with the regulations in each of the countries concerned e.g., food safety, electronic devices etc., – think cost and time as this can be an onerous task for small businesses.

Furthermore, smart, workable, business systems and processes will need to be designed, developed, and implemented – these can be refined as the business evolves.

The list seems endless. The reality is entrepreneurs, regardless of age and stage, constantly juggle their tasks and time every day – working both on the business, and in the business. If they have access to little or no support, they literally wear all the hats, and need to manage their energy and productivity. Recognising that we all age differently, and appreciating there are many contributing factors, we generally have less energy as we age than we had previously. If we understand and manage our energy levels, we can focus on our goals, tune into our strengths, become aware of, and accept our limitations, and reach out for support to deal with the challenges we encounter along the way.

Learning as we go, incompatible strands of the business soon become evident. For example, passion in a time-consuming project may not generate a sustainable source of income. Traveling long distances to undertake short work assignments may not be profitable. Cliff wanted variety in his business – hence the three strands: Lawn mowing, handman services, and security services. In practice he found the handyman tasks often turned into much bigger jobs that took more time than had been anticipated for little reward. The security side of his business, (which was more interesting), didn't fit with his lawn mowing schedule as the latter was weather dependent. Learning from his experience Cliff refined his services, and later sold his lawnmowing business to develop his security business.

Mark and Sone made a deliberate decision to develop three products. "It's easier for people to make a decision". They love doing the markets as they enjoy personal interaction with their customers and therefore will continue to do this. Their strategy for expansion is to sell their three sauces directly to speciality grocery stores, cafes, restaurants, gastro pubs and supermarkets, and to offer consumers complimentary recipes. Mark and Sone hire casuals to help them make their sauces on an 'as needs' basis.

Phil's business 'Eco Shifter' expanded rapidly. Initially he was a one-man-band. As the demand for his services increased both locally and further afield, his own hours of work expanded to meet the needs of his customers. To overcome this challenge, he gradually took on staff, trained them and purchased more vehicles. Contemplating the longer term, Phil considered taking on more staff, and/or franchising his business. "I investigated the possibilities and decided to franchise. As a franchisor I can grow the company and help others go into business. As I've set up and worked in the business myself, I can guide and mentor franchisees to be successful. It's a win/win situation. When I started out, I didn't know I'd be going down this route".

Juggling time, energy, family, and community commitments alongside your business commitments can be challenging. Liz said, "It always takes longer than you think to set up a business, develop it and build a reputation. It takes about five years to get a business off the ground. Don't get impatient. It can be a long slow grind but keep at it when faced with brick walls. Be openminded for opportunities. Start small. Don't be frugal with your investment. Bite the bullet and do it properly, and make sure you have the budget to back up what you are doing until your business gets established".

In summary, plan your work, and work your plan. Set goals. Make a list, focus on what you can do, how you will achieve it, and have a deadline. Manage your time, energy, and productivity. If you cannot do all the tasks yourself, (think quality, consistency, and timeliness), seek support or outsource these tasks to someone who has the skills to do this for you.

Marketing

Marketing is at the heart of all businesses. Most solo entrepreneurs and small businesses specialise in offering products and services that leverage our interest, personal skills, and expertise, but we tend to struggle when it comes to marketing. It's a skill most of us must learn from scratch and the very thought of this can be overwhelming. It's evident that we need to effectively market our products and services to potential customers for them to buy them. Whether we choose to undertake this task ourselves, or outsource the responsibility to someone else, this critical aspect of running a business requires a workable marketing plan. Developing and executing this plan requires time, resources, and a budget.

Common pain points for entrepreneurs about marketing are: -

1. Learning to value yourself – putting a price on your products and your services. This is a biggie.
2. Insufficient clarity re your target market. Who are the customers you are trying to attract?
3. Not knowing how to reach your target market. Where are your potential clients, and how do they shop? You don't have to be everywhere – you just need to be where your current, and potential customers can see you, and offer them what they want.
4. No marketing plan – no specific measurable marketing goals in the short and the longer-term for your business, with deadlines for achieving them.
5. Not enough time (or inclination) - to develop marketing campaigns, to select the appropriate media, and develop content messaging.
6. Inadequate time, inclination, or confidence - spent on implementing your marketing plan, to promote your products/service, to create, grow, and maintain your customer base, and to measure your results. What's working and what isn't.
7. Little or no marketing budget. Effective marketing doesn't have to cost an arm and a leg, but it does require an investment in your business to get results.
8. Not confident with technology – e.g., to develop and manage your website, social media etc. It's a learning curve. Familiarise yourself with online technology and

> choose the platforms that work for you. Hire the best to develop your website. For more information check out **Digital Boost Alliance Aotearoa | Helping accelerate the use of digital technologies in Aotearoa | DigitalBoost**

9. No system in place to maintain contact with your customers and prospective customers. You need a process in place to keep in touch - at least monthly. It works like magic (e.g., phone calls, emails, newsletters, thank you cards, invitations, and events).

10. Untimely or no response to enquiries and requests via phone calls, emails, texts, complaints etc. This is disrespectful and erodes trust. We've all experienced 'the black hole' when we've left messages for people in what appears to be 'cyber space'. It doesn't leave a good impression. Courtesy goes a long way. A prompt response to enquiries and requests shows that you care about the person concerned and are reliable. Think consistency and trust and build loyalty with your customers for your products and service.

Approaches to marketing, and the media selected to attract clients varies from business to business. However, the common pain points listed in this section are generic and can be used as a checklist for reflecting on your own marketing learning journey. As you read through this section, think about your strengths, and note where improvements can be made?

Marketing your Business

Marketing is vital to the success of your business. You don't have to be an expert, but you do need to be clear on your marketing strategy, work to a plan, measure what's working and what isn't, and based on the results act in real time. If marketing isn't one of your strengths, delegate it to someone who understands your business and is better equipped to do the job but don't forget to monitor the activity and track performance.

Business is a people dealing with people activity. As you know more about your business than anyone else, you are in the best position to talk about it. This isn't a mechanical act, or a 'hard sell', and it's important to remember that business is reciprocal. Every interaction with another person makes an impression either favourable or unfavourable and this includes appearance. Appearance and first impressions matter. People want to do business with people they 'know, like and trust'. Additional key attributes that help to attract people and opportunities include a friendly personality, good manners, and politeness. Self-confidence, enthusiasm, and well-developed listening, written and verbal communication skills are also important. It pays to invest in developing these skills.

Growing your business means making new contacts every week. When meeting with new contacts you have a very short window of opportunity to share the essence of what you do and why someone needs your services. You know what you do, but can you explain it succinctly? Are you prepared to explain your vision repeatedly in different contexts to different audiences? And – the biggie, are you comfortable facing rejection? Regardless of how good your products and services are, not everyone will want to purchase them.

This is a good time to define and freshen up your elevator pitch. This pitch is a concise speech used to sell yourself, your business, and/or your product and services in a very short space of time - the time it takes to get from one floor to another in an elevator, without lecturing or boring the pants off the person you are sharing the lift with. Is it time to freshen up your elevator pitch?

Five steps to describe your product or service simply and easily in a snap!

1. My name, and the business I'm in.
2. My products and/or service.
3. The problem I'm trying to solve, the opportunities I offer, and the benefits – what my product and/or service helps people to achieve, and the feelings it provides (e.g., peace of mind).
4. What makes me the best   how do I stand out from the crowd.
5. How can people contact me.

Keep it short 60 seconds or less - 80-100 words. Speak with confidence and make it interesting to your audience. Vary your elevator pitch depending on your audience. This means you will need several versions. Experiment. Try it out with people in your network. Seek their feedback and find out what works for you.

It pays to invest in your people skills, and when hiring staff or outsourcing any aspect of your business, be sure to hire people with these skills to work with you. If you employ staff, help them to develop and practice their elevator pitch. A consistent approach builds trust and loyalty and reinforces the message about your products/services and the way in which you conduct your business. Here is an example of Richard Calkin's elevator pitch.

"I'm Richard Calkin, Founder of Web Genius, where we help kiwi business heroes harness the power of the internet to generate more customers, and more repeat business."

Check out Richard's website for more information. (Web Design Auckland Wellington Christchurch Dunedin | Websites NZ (webgenius.co.nz)).

Pricing your Products and Services

When she went into business, Cathy quickly found that to provide value to someone else, you must first value yourself. This includes your expertise, your products and services, your time, and the journey that you are on. Pricing your products and service is critically important to the viability of your business, and it's a topic that is frequently discussed when networking with other entrepreneurs. Research and analysis will help you to:

- Calculate the cost of running your business – this includes the cost of each of your products and services, and all of your expenses associated with this, including your salary, and your overheads.
- Come up with a pricing strategy, and
- Minimise the potential to make unnecessary, and expensive mistakes.

One of the most common ways to set your pricing schedule for your business is to know your competition. But it's not the only strategy. Consider the following: -

1. What is the going rate for my product and/or service?
2. How does what I offer compare with similar products of services offered by others in terms of quality, expertise, and service?
3. What is my point of difference? What is my value proposition, the tangible and intangible benefits I offer for

my ideal customers? What are my products and services worth to them?

4. How will I determine a realistic starting price – not so low that I kill my margins, and not so high that my product/service is out of reach for my clients?

5. How can I be upfront and transparent about the price of my products/service.

Don't forget to increase your price in steady increments as your costs increase, and your experience grows. And always respond swiftly to changes in the market.

Three further tips on this topic: -

1. The research and analysis process is ongoing – not a once only task.

2. It's always easier to lower your prices than to increase them.

3. If you are not confident pricing your products and services, seek advice.

Promoting your business

There are so many ways you can promote your business, your products, and your services. Here are a few for you to consider: -

1. Advertisements in newspapers and magazines,
2. Articles in newspapers and magazines,
3. Letters to the editor,
4. Websites,
5. Brochures,
6. Blogs on your website, and/or other people's websites,
7. Social media campaigns,

8. Newsletters,
9. Speaking engagements,
10. Exhibitions,
11. Radio/TV interviews,
12. Workshops – face-to-face and/or online,
13. Posters – on community noticeboards, in shop windows, and on billboards,
14. Videos/YouTube,
15. Sample products,
16. Useful gifts,
17. Events,
18. Books,
19. Banners,
20. Local markets.

Be selective – don't try to do them all. Only choose two or three platforms that are affordable and speak to your audience. Develop a marketing plan that you can manage and monitor. You don't have to be everywhere, but you need to be visible where your existing, and potential customers can see you.

Small business trends suggest that there is a correlation between the amount of time spent on marketing and the growth of the business (58 Percent of Small Businesses Spend 5 Hours or Less on Marketing (smallbiztrends.com)). It is very difficult to put a timeframe on this activity, as individual skills and approaches to the task vary. As a rough guide, approximately 22% of small businesses spend between 5-10 hours per week on this activity, and a further 10% invested more time to get the desired results.

Consider the following: -

- What marketing media am I most comfortable with?

- How much time am I spending on this activity, and how much time am I prepared to spend on this activity?
- What is my marketing budget and how is this spent?
- What's working for me what isn't? How often do I measure this, and based on the results, what action am I taking?

Consistency and frequency in messaging is also important. Remember to offer your clients what they want and tell them how they can get it – repeatedly. Although you have said and heard the message numerous times, there is an adage in marketing called 'The Rule of 7'. Translated this means the message needs to be said at least seven times in print, digital and verbal communication before it sticks with the consumer. Disciplined repetition is key.

Ask yourself: -

- How consistent is your messaging?
- What is the frequency of your messaging?

When writing content to promote your products and service to potential customers, consider using the AIDA model to help you craft your advertisement.

1. Attention - create a compelling headline to attract their attention.
2. Interest - provide details of your products/services, price etc. to create interest in them
3. Desire - describe the benefits of your products/services to your customers to stimulate their desire to want them.
4. Action – a compelling call to action e.g., special offer, last chance etc. to purchase your products/service – now.

If you'd like more tips on marketing, check out this article and consider joining Digital Boost, which offers support to small business owners to digitally transform their operating models. Check out this website for more details Digital Boost™ | Ministry of Business, Innovation & Employment (mbie.govt.nz)

Compliance with Regulations, Certification, Licensing and Quality Management Systems

All businesses in New Zealand must work within the regulatory environment. In addition, businesses that manufacture products in New Zealand, must comply with specific regulations and go through a process to gain the requisite certification. Businesses that export products overseas, must also comply with the regulatory framework for each of the countries they distribute to – which varies from country to country. If you have no previous experience, this can be challenging, but not impossible. Like everything else, it's a learning curve, and it pays to get timely and appropriate advice.

Here are some examples: -

- Mark and Sone Edwards had to fulfil the requirements of the food safety regulations to make and sell their sauces. This included building a dedicated, separate purpose-built kitchen for their business, and having food safety inspections and certification, and documented processes in place.
- Richard Eltherington manufactures and distributes natural health products and therefore must also comply with food safety regulations in New Zealand. As Richard's business

exports products overseas, he also must meet the requirements for each of the countries he distributes to.

- Kareen Holland manufacturers an extensive range of natural and organics skincare products. She gained GMP Certification (good manufacturing practice certification) - proof that Kareen consistently produces, tests, and packages her products from whoa to go using robust operating procedures until they reach the point of use in accordance with quality standards.

- Karen and Stephen (Dri-sleeper), manufacture a range of products in their business, which includes, but is not limited to electronic devices – these must comply with the requisite regulations in New Zealand. As Dri-sleeper exports overseas, this business also must meet the rules and regulations that vary for each country they distribute to.

Compliance with regulations, certification, and licencing to sell these products requires a documented quality management system and businesses are audited to ensure they comply. For a small business this can be an onerous task, expensive, and time consuming. Like many, Karen had no prior experience in exporting products overseas. The learning process involved lots of discussion and lobbying – but pays dividends. Dri-sleeper now services clients in Europe, the USA, UK, Canada, and Asia.

Importers (such as Marie Hannan's business – the Nepal-New Zealand Connection), must also comply with regulations, meet biosecurity standards and if importing food, must register with the Ministry of Primary Industries as a food importer. Furthermore, all commercially imported goods must be cleared through the New Zealand Customs Service and incur Customs duties and Good and Service Tax.

To reiterate, for those who have no previous experience, understanding and complying with regulations, gaining the necessary certification and licences, and developing and implementing quality management systems can be challenging. However, the entrepreneurs that feature in this book demonstrate that these challenges are not insurmountable. It's a learning curve, and it pays to get timely and appropriate advice.

Managing Risk – Business Systems, Intellectual Property, Ideas etc.

Unfortunately, despite taking all precautionary measures, including internal controls, there are occasions when business ideas, products and services, systems, methods, policies, and practices, are 'borrowed', 'stolen', 'copied', and/or 'modified', without permission. In situations like these, individuals and/or colleagues, once associated with your business, tap into what I would call your 'intellectual property' and using this, openly form their own business in competition with you. Some go so far as to take your customers with them.

Ken Shilling shared a couple of examples of this from his own experience with two separate businesses. The first was 'Guildcraft Projects with Trades' in Wellington. You'll recall this was a franchise operation. Ken as the franchisor developed a system whereby, he mentored, trained, and supported a collective group of highly skilled craftsmen (franchisees), and was able to provide cost efficiencies for tools and supplies for the members. It was a very successful business model. But, but over time, equipped with their knowledge, skills, experience and contacts, franchisees could no longer see the value of being part of the bigger group and elected to form their own independent businesses. 'Guildcraft Projects with Trades' was no longer a viable concern, and the Shillings closed the business down and invested their energy and expertise elsewhere. Subsequently some of the breakaway tradespeople were successful as independent operators. Others, lacking the structure, support, and mentorship of the professional body, weren't as lucky.

The second example is the expansion of the Shilling's 'Link Technology' business into Australia. You'll recall, a local master agent was recruited and trained to act using the same software and processes. Once again, the venture was very successful, but unfortunately, and almost like the Guildcraft experience, the master agent determined that they now had the knowledge base, (which in this case would include the integrated system and processes), and the established customer base to go it alone. Rather than get into a lengthy and expensive dispute, the Shillings wisely shut the Australian based business down and the legal association with the master agent was terminated.

Learning from these experiences, Ken said he would never own a franchise operation again. The good news is that the Shilling's later set up a new business in Melbourne and managed to retain some of their customers. His advice is to others is: -

"Trust no one, embrace change, associate with the best, and never give up"

Cyber-crime

Increasingly small businesses are at risk of malicious cyber-attacks. While technology makes it easier to do business online, it also makes us more vulnerable to cyber threats. Since the onset of the pandemic, which has impacted the way in which we work, there has been a huge surge in cybercrime on a global scale. Cyber-attacks occur when cyber criminals gain illegal access to electronic data stored on computers and the networks associated with them and disrupt or control the system, steal sensitive information including customer data and wreak havoc on your business and bank account.

In brief, common cyber threats include, but are not limited to:-

- Phishing scams – usually by phone, text messaging, email, or social media, where individuals are lured with a sense of urgency into providing information e.g., bank and credit card details, account details, passwords etc. This cyber-attack can result in identity and financial theft.
- Malware – malicious software, e.g., viruses and worms, which cause operational issues, data loss, and spread from system to system. And spyware that reveals sensitive information including passwords.
- Ransomware – malicious software that encrypts information, denying you access to it. A demand for financial payment ensues before the data may (or may not) be released back to you.
- Insider threat – these come from people within the business. These can be employees or former employees, contractors, partners, or business associates that have inside information about your business practices, systems, intellectual property, and data, etc. Insider threats can be costly and obliterate a lifetime's work in an instant.

In addition to the identified threats, cyber-attacks may cause privacy breaches (e.g., unauthorised distribution of client information). Apart from business disruption, the main risks are financial, legal, and damage to your reputation - from which it is difficult to recover.

The best way for entrepreneurs to protect themselves is to: -

- Increase awareness of cyber-attacks.
- Institute simple procedures to reduce human error and build resilience.
- Invest in good anti-virus software and security to protect your business.
- Instigate back-up measures to minimise the impact of a cyber-attack.

To summarise, we've explored the most common problems shared by entrepreneurs who started their business @ 50+ - excluding the impact of COVID, which we'll discuss in the next chapter. In response to some of these challenges useful tips have been offered that may be useful for those of you who have recently started or are planning to start a business. Overall, we can learn from another's experiences, especially if they have been on a similar journey themselves.

It also pays to be proactive and get a Business Mentor. Seeking expert help will set you up for success and save you time and money in the long run. (Check out www.businessmentors.org.nz). For more than 30 years, this service has been matching experienced businesspeople, (the Mentors), with small business owners, (the Mentees), including start-up entrepreneurs. It's also prudent to invest in expert and timely financial, legal, and IT advice.

9 The Impact of COVID

There is no disputing the fact that everyone's life has been impacted by the global pandemic. Worldwide, restrictive measures were introduced, in an effort to slow down and minimise the spread of the aggressive, deadly, virus and manage the devasting effects on humanity. In response to the nature and scale of the crisis, every aspect of our lives drastically changed, literally overnight. Inevitably, the lockdowns and restrictions caused massive social and economic disruption on a global scale. Everything in our lives came to a grinding halt. Even the postal service, a service we trusted and took for granted for hundreds of years, came to a standstill, and has never recovered. The world of work and lifestyles significantly changed.

Small businesses were extremely vulnerable. Without question, the pandemic was by far the biggest challenge the entrepreneurs who feature in this book faced. There was no contingency plan.

Fortunately, the New Zealand government offered financial and other support to small businesses, which included sole traders, contractors, self-employed people, businesses with employees and registered charities. This support included: -

- Low-interest loans,
- Tax refunds,
- Payments for people who suddenly became unemployed,
- Income relief payments, and
- Support for dealing with creditors, commercial landlords, and/or business tenants. New rules were introduced allowing COVID-19 impacted businesses to temporarily

place existing debt into 'hibernation', with the agreement of 50% of their creditors, until they were to start trading normally again.

It took time for these measures to be implemented, and strict eligibility criteria was introduced, for example businesses had to declare their viability and that the money allocated would be used for core operating costs. For various reasons, some businesses in New Zealand did not seek financial support during the height of the pandemic.

In this chapter we'll focus on the impact of the pandemic on the entrepreneurs who feature in this book, and the steps they took to manage the situation.

For Denise's business, Helping Hand African Tours, and Safari's, the impact of the pandemic was devasting. When the international borders closed, tours were cancelled, money had to be refunded, and her business came to a complete standstill. This also impacted on the businesses of her African co-workers in Kenya and Uganda, and her associates in Australia. There was no way of knowing how long the pandemic was going to last, and when the restrictions would be lifted. Initially filled with hope, as the months dragged on it became clear to Denise that life, as we knew it, would not be returning to the 'new normal' any time soon. Reluctantly accepting the situation, but firmly committed to her WHY, she made the decision to put Helping Hand African Tours and Safari's 'on hold' rather than quit her business. Over the months, that turned into years, Denise remained in regular contact with her clients and her colleagues on both continents.

Meanwhile, instead of lamenting her loss, Denise maintained her business networks in New Zealand, and channelled her energy elsewhere. A serial entrepreneur at heart, she is not afraid to try things out and give things a go. Refocusing her attention and energy, she pursued several other innovative business ideas, always accepting that some ideas will work, and some won't. Utilising her creative strengths, she invested her time in creative pursuits and generated a stream of income, knowing that these side hustles were temporary measures. Eventually she hit on the swimwear idea and her 'Kailani Pearl Swim' business was born, and this business is congruent with Helping Hand African Tours and Safari's. Had it not been for the pandemic, Denise may never have gone down this track.

The pandemic hit Richard's health and wellbeing business hard. As international travel was curbed, planned travel to trade shows, including the biggest natural food trade show in Anaheim, where 20,000 companies are profiled, was impossible for Richard. He and his family have invested heavily in Healthy Start (NZ) Ltd. They'd met the regulatory requirements and gained the requisite approvals from various countries to market and distribute their products on a global scale – no mean feat. Having a presence at major international events, and with that the opportunity to establish business connections with others in this industry was key to becoming known in this sector. Whilst it was extremely frustrating, Richard remained focused, maintained his networks, and focused his efforts on marketing and online distribution.

When the borders re-opened, pre-departure test requirements and extended stays in managed isolation and quarantine facilities were instituted in New Zealand, and similar steps were taken elsewhere. The question that Richard and others in this situation asked themselves before travelling was, "What happens if I get stranded while I'm away"? With plans in place, it was a risk

Richard was prepared to take and he was ready to roll with it.

During the worst of the pandemic, Marie couldn't import the stock for her shop from Nepal. She also worried about the villagers she had come to know as she had lived amongst them for four years prior to returning to New Zealand. "COVID hit us hard, but how would they manage in these circumstances? There is no other way they can sell their goods. The stock that was in transit to New Zealand was held up in various countries along the way. Even when it arrived in Auckland, there were huge delays, as this district was in lockdown much longer than other destinations in New Zealand". Marie's imported goods were not regarded as, 'essential products or services', and therefore were not prioritised for transportation. Local open-air markets were not functioning as there were restrictions on the number of people at gatherings. Marie, who was comfortable using social media, upped her online marketing and sales during this period.

Jules also changed tack and moved her Tupperware parties online. "The virus made me think differently, and Tupperware gave us the tools to operate in an online world". Inevitably people became isolated during the lockdowns. This didn't lighten up when new regimes were later introduced with different 'rules' for the vaccinated and the unvaccinated. Restrictions were introduced limiting the number of people that could gather in public places – making some business and social events unworkable. People looked for alternative ways to socialise and to do business, most of which was managed from our own homes. Suddenly geographic location had no bearing when it came to online Tupperware parties. Individuals could take part regardless of where they lived, and as a result this strategy was hugely successful. Attendees got to meet new people face-to-face online, socialise and have fun, learn something new, and shop. It was a win/win situation.

Suz Stokes (35-Day Detox) had been in business for several years when COVID hit. Technically savvy, Suz was already sharing her work online. Unable to facilitate classes in her yoga studio during the lockdowns, Suz, focused her efforts on redesigning her website, and developed numerous useful videos and blogs to make it easier for her clients to access the benefits of the 35 Day Detox programme regardless of where they are in the world. She also redecorated her studio ready to re-open for her clients when the restrictions were lifted.

The impact of the pandemic in terms of loss of life, livelihoods, social connections, access to medical services, restrictions regarding funerals, weddings etc. the list goes on, severely increased the stress levels of the population worldwide. During the crisis, Tony Yuile knew people desperately needed what he had to offer. He proactively kept in contact with his existing client base by phone and e.mail but potential clients – the stressed, anxious, and depressed, were hard to reach – even online.

Chirpy Plus's mission to 'eliminate loneliness and social isolation in people aged 50 and over, by providing them with a safe and easy way to make new friends' was thwarted during the pandemic. The very people they were servicing – many of whom are older, and live alone, were the most vulnerable to the deadly virus. Isolated during the lockdowns, there wasn't the opportunity to 'chirp' with their community and join in the activities in the way they were accustomed to. Although zoom meetings were a godsend, not everyone is familiar with the technology and confident in using it. Carol and Shaun remained positive and focused and kept the communication channels open with their network of volunteer hosts and their members.

Like many, I was stunned when we went into our first lockdown at midnight on 25th March 2020. Workshops were cancelled, and the launch event for my first book 'Life On Our Own Terms', scheduled to be held two days later, was cancelled. Several months later, when the restrictions were lifted, the book was launched - but the momentum was lost. I launched the second book in the Older and Bolder series later that year. The restrictions limited the number of people who could gather in one place for the event, and safe social distancing measures were in place. For obvious reasons, people were reluctant to participate in social activities. Talk about things coming in threes – in August 2021, another nation-wide lockdown was announced, days before the planned launch for my third book in the series. Whilst appreciating the need for the lockdowns, the experience was demoralising, especially for people who featured in the books and for the communities associated with them. Like others, I kept the communication channels open with my network, and whenever possible, honoured the speaking engagements I had agreed to. During this extended period, I spent much of my time publishing my own projects and writing blogs and training courses for my clients.

Several businesses were in the early stage of establishment when COVID hit. Jan Thornborough (Intelligensia) literally left her job one day and went into lockdown the next. Not much you can do about that, except focus on developing your business and growing your network online.

Tom Rodden (Peak Coaching) had just moved to Taranaki when COVID struck. He joined online networks, and kept himself busy writing an e.book and articles for magazines.

Heather Knewstubb (Time Genie) invested in her own development by getting a business coach, who helped her to find her niche. Through the process she identified the type of work she really wanted to focus on, that fully utilised her skills and experience, and narrowed down the client group she wanted to work with. "I wanted to work with interesting, creative people who are passionate about what they do, and recognise they can't do everything themselves". This experience enabled Heather's business to evolve and grow.   She now undertakes stimulating, intellectually challenging work with a variety of clients, both in New Zealand and Australia, which is very rewarding.

The impact of the pandemic wasn't as catastrophic for Dri-Sleeper, as most of their clients like to shop online, and the systems and processes were already established.

The hardest thing for many was to remain positive, focus on the tasks that were within our control and keep up the momentum. Whilst the impact of COVID has been very challenging for everyone, and clearly had a huge economic and social impact, the experience provided the opportunity to step back from our busy lives. We suddenly had the chance to reflect and reconsider who and what is important to us, and how we spend our time. In a turmoil, our lives were turned upside down, we had the unexpected opportunity to change gears, to: -

- Read, learn, and grow.
- Expand our imagination.
- Develop our skills, products, and services.
- Reconnect with family and clients in a different way.
- Pursue creative activities.
- Focus on health and wellbeing and build resilience.
- Develop new perspectives.

- Reflect on our achievements.
- Refresh our plans.
- Revise outdated and unnecessary systems and processes.
- Appreciate a more balanced lifestyle, and so much more.

Launching a business can be challenging at the best of times. Launching and managing a business during a global pandemic is a remarkable feat, requiring a high level of emotional agility and effort. With a greater sense of strength, resilience, optimism, and creativity, we've all had to tweak, modify, and adapt in one way or another. Experiencing and dealing with challenges as they arise, stretches us, and shows us just how much we are capable of.

In his book 'Flow' Mihaly Csikszentmihalyi sums it up:

"The best moments in our lives are not the passive, receptive relaxing times. The best moments usually occur when a person's body or mind is stretched to its limits in a voluntary effort to accomplish something difficult and worthwhile".

Awesome!

While the pandemic had a catastrophic impact around the globe, there have also been some positive outcomes. For example: -

- People have become more resourceful.
- We have had the opportunity to take time out to learn new skills.
- Through the difficult times we've learned to appreciate what we do have including our families and friends.
- Technology has changed the way we do business and interact with one another (e.g., working from home, zoom meetings).

- We've also had the time to reflect on what really matters to us, and how we spend our time, and this includes the nature of our work.

Astonishingly, since the onset of COVID-19 pandemic, more people than ever before are starting a business for the first time in later life. According to the Office for Seniors in New Zealand, self-employment income for older people is projected to increase from $3.98 billion in 2021 to an incredible $17.19 billion by 2071. How exciting is that!

Nevertheless, there is no room for complacency.

Business Contingency Planning

It's unlikely any business had a contingency plan for a two-plus year pandemic, and there are lessons to be learned from the experience. It begs the question: -

How many small businesses have a back-up plan to ensure the business can continue to operate in the event of any natural disaster, major technical issues including prolonged power cuts, or any other unexpected event?

In New Zealand, the most common natural disasters that occur are earthquakes, floods, bushfires, cyclones, landslides, and droughts – and we have active volcanos. In 2022, in the wake of the pandemic, tornadoes, torrential rain, floods, and fires have wreaked havoc in Aotearoa. Every business, including small businesses, needs a contingency plan that outlines potential risks to all aspects of the business. This includes but is not limited to products, services, customers, suppliers, and equipment – including technology, and details of your insurance. The actions that will be taken to keep the business running need to be outlined, including potential relocation to alternative premises and a communication plan.

Learning from the impact of the pandemic, loss of revenue, loss of customers, and increased expenses need to be factored in.

It pays to be prepared. Should a disruption occur, you'll know what to do and will be able to take swift action. The easiest way to develop a contingency plan is to use a template.

(TEMPLATE-Business-Continuity-Plan.pdf (getprepared.nz)).

10 Looking to the Future

Regardless of age and stage, we've learned that starting a business requires energy, enthusiasm, and determination, as well as courage and resilience in the face of adversity. We've also learned that it's never too late to change gears, consider new options, possibilities, and adventures, or get started on what you secretly wanted to do. The opportunities are limitless.

Although the challenges, trials and tribulations were many and varied, without exception, all the entrepreneurs interviewed for this book stepped outside of their comfort zone and embarked on a learning journey. They are all excited about the path they are on and the lifestyle they have created for themselves. Energised with what they have accomplished, they are all looking forward to what the future holds. These individuals also offer words of encouragement for those embarking on a similar path.

In his early 70's John Skene (Aviation History Advocate), is looking forward to what's coming next, ***"I feel like I'm just getting started,"*** he said.

Karen and Stephen, from Dri-Sleeper believe, ***"The options are limitless".*** Their advice to others, ***"Get comfortable with the digital world. Develop an undefeatable human spirit - persist tirelessly".***

Audiologist Jeanie Morrison-Low enjoys making a living doing what she loves and she's good at it. A creative person, she applies scientific knowledge with artistry, makes her own decisions, and gets good results for her clients. ***"I meet and help an array of people to live happier lives".*** Her advice, ***"Find you 'Ikigai' –***

your life purpose and go for it"

The impact of COVID wasn't as drastic on Phil Byrne's Eco-Shifter business, as it was for other types of businesses. During the lockdown, many people spent their time clearing out their homes and garages. There was plenty of stuff to be taken to the charity shops and recycling areas when these re-opened for business. Houses came and went on the market, and with that furniture and possessions had to be moved from one place to another. In the aftermath of the pandemic, Phil's business has expanded. He's established one franchise, and more are on the horizon.

From Phil's perspective, Winston Churchill's quote hits the mark,

"Success is not final, failure is not fatal, it's the courage to continue that counts".

Annette from The Inner Path is passionate about what she offers and the outcomes she has attained. Inspired in her work, she's published an e.Book entitled 'The Hidden Trauma', which is available on her website (The Inner Path | Be your true self | Feel alive and happy).

Annette says, ***"Trust yourself. If it feels right, give it a go".*** This was her biggest lesson and the best advice.

Fully utilising her skills, Suz from 35-Day Detox continues to push the boundaries and is now offering her health and wellbeing expertise and development programmes in the workplace. Suz's book, is available on Amazon in Kindle and paperback formats. (The Physical Manifestation of Self: High Heels to Yoga Pants, with a side of IRONMAN : Stokes, Suz H: Amazon.com.au: Books).

In addition to his private practice, Tony Yuile is teaching at the

New Zealand School of Hypnotherapy. His book, '7 Ways to Reduce Anxiety in 7 Minutes or Less' is available on Amazon in Kindle and paperback formats. (7 Ways To Reduce Anxiety In 7 Minutes Or Less: Think clearly, feel relaxed and perform at your best under pressure : Yuile, Tony: Amazon.com.au: Books).

Tony's advice, ***"People make choices. Take control. Don't let others make them for you".***

Looking to the future Helen Hancox, from No Nonsense Networker doesn't accept excuses. ***"We all make choices on how we spend our time. We can fumble through spinning our wheels, or we can stay in our zone of genius and seek support when we need it. Accountability is key"*** – and Helen should know. In her global online business, she is very selective about who she works with. ***"I only work with those who are committed, accountable, and strive to achieve results".***

Helen's advice, ***"We all make choices on how we spend our time. Don't make excuses. Be accountable to yourself, and to others".***

"Despite the challenges – you've just got to believe in your WHY and excited about WHAT you do", said Denise Carnihan. Adventurous as ever, she is fired up about the future. As soon as the international border reopened, Denise and her husband rescheduled the tours they were going to run before the outbreak of the pandemic. Denise and Chris are hosting two fully booked parallel tours simultaneously to Kenya to accommodate their clients, and a third tour is planned. Meanwhile, her Kailani Pearl swimwear range and accessories for mature women, that are available in bold, bright patterns, have been a huge success. It's incredible what can be achieved when you have an idea and are galvanised into action to make it happen. And……this range of swimwear is all made from recycled ocean waste.

Denise's advice, *"I'm a big believer in the here and now. Be spontaneous. Grab the opportunities. Do your research and just do it. Go for it"!*

Working from home became an acceptable way of operating for most organisations during the pandemic. With the passing of time, flexible ways of working have been introduced as the 'new normal'. These factors are what some individuals wanted when they started up their business in the first place. In a few short years, despite the pandemic, Cliff Gott has set up two successful, owner operated businesses, one of which he has since sold – during the pandemic. Constantly learning and applying new skills, Cliff has developed his own newsletter and writes blogs about the services he provides for his Secure Time clients. He's also developed his skills and increased his presence on social media (www.facebook.com/stsecuretime).

Cliff's advice, *"Take action. Talk to people. Do your research and give your idea a go. Take the first step, and then the next. Don't struggle with what you can't do yourself – outsource this to an expert (e.g., a website)".*

Cliff's favourite quote came from Henry Ford.

"Whether you think you can, or you can't, you're right".

A nationwide lockdown was announced on Jan Thornborough's first day in her own cyber security business. It was a terrifyingly shaky start. But she knew she wasn't alone, and all things come to pass. During the lockdowns, and in the time since, more people are online, including the cyber attackers. Engaged in a massive programme to educate small and medium sized businesses to build resilience she is expanding her own business and taking on staff to achieve her mission.

Jan's advice, *"Look before you leap. Do your research. Investigate and make a list of potential businesses/clients. Look at the long-term. Take calculated risks".*

Likewise, Raewynne Graf recommends others to, *"Do your homework. Ensuring there is a viable opportunity in the industry you chose. Don't take on the concept that because you are over a certain age you should 'retire' - ask yourself 'retiring from what'? Be prepared to take a few knock backs and build resilience to be a forward thinker. Keep your vision always at the fore, and when things get tough, just go back to your plan, and reconnect with the dream/product - your 'Why'. Ask yourself, 'What you are doing all this for'? Share you good times and celebrate the small successes you have experienced on your journey and final, learn from the barriers you are forced to get over or mistakes made on the way".*

Rosemary Emery and Anne Russell are passionate about what they do and have years of specialised experience in the field. Their fully self-funded business has grown exponentially. The website is being refreshed and with the development of a new app, Off the Page is on track to broaden its reach and provide better access to their resources. They are meeting the need of older emergent readers, and the teachers and parents of young adults with special needs and or reading difficulties. They focus their resources on teaching these young adults invaluable life skills, they can relate to.

Their advice, *"Persevere".*

Focused on living his own life to the max and ensuring natural health products are available worldwide to enable others to do the same, Richard Eltherington is relentless in his efforts to go global with Healthy Start. *"We can manufacture and supply natural health products from New Zealand. We have an amazing natural environment and exceptionally high standards surrounding the production and processing of food products. But we are a small consumer market. We are going global and will do whatever it takes"*.

Richard's advice to others, *"Everyone should have the best life they can. Don't wait. Do it. Give it a go. Live life to the max"!*

Andrew Burn (ERP 365) is excited about the future, especially for his clients in food manufacturing, importing and distribution. Taking a personalised approach, he helps his clients to implement improved business process automation in a people friendly way, enabling the business to thrive and grow.

Andrew's advice, *"Stay true to yourself, who and what you are. Listen to the feedback. Take forward what you've learned in the past and operate in a flexible, balanced, and modern way. Be open to new knowledge – don't just rush in. Sometimes the longer road is the shorter road. People see what you do. I always have tomorrow planned. As an entrepreneur you are your own motivator. There is nothing quite like getting your hands dirty. Get to know your customers. Sit with them and their staff. Find out what they like and what annoys them about the system, and work to resolve their issues"*.

Liz has a track record of success in business. Starting her new Enrich Retirement business in her mid-60's, Liz is inspired by a quote by Paul J Meyer.

"Whatever you vividly imagine, ardently desire, sincerely believe, and enthusiastically act upon must inevitably come to pass"

Powerful words that can be taken to heart, regardless of the barriers we may face.

Her advice to others venturing out on their own is to, ***"Give your business time. Don't expect overnight success. It takes five years to get a business off the ground. Don't get impatient. It can be a long slow grind and you must keep at it when faced with brick walls. Be open minded for opportunities. Start small but invest the money in your investment and have enough dollars to back up what you're doing until it gets established. Don't do your business frugally. Bite the bullet and do it properly"***.

The impact of the pandemic clearly prompted more businesses to offer their products and services online, and consumers embraced this way of shopping and engaging with others during the lockdowns. Who'd have thought that people would engage in online Tupperware parties. Jules Fitzgerald loves the flexibility in the way in which she provides her service whether it's one-on-one advice (provided either online or in person), cooking and storage demonstrations for groups of 2-4 people or parties for larger groups. Genevieve McLachlan also facilitates online classes, providing advice on the use of essential oils.

Genevieve McLachlan's offers advice from the heart to those who are thinking about starting a business, ***"It's not about finance, it's about passion"***.

Having put in the hard yards, Kareen Holland's business - Kd One Skincare and Cosmetics is well established with a strong brand

and reputation. As sole owner operator, Kareen manages the manufacturing, retail and wholesale aspects of her business and provides beauty treatment for her clients. Over time, she has seen a lot of people come and go in business.

Kareen's advice to others embarking on this path is, *"You've got to get out and do it in a way that works for you".*

Strengthening Community Connection, Cohesion and Resilience

Although technology allowed us to speak with friends and family all over the world, not everyone has access, or makes use of it. During the lockdowns, families were separated, domestic and international travel was curbed, and there was controversy regarding the vaccination regimes. Apart from the economic impact, many people felt isolated, alone, and anxious about catching the deadly virus. For some individual's days, or weeks could go by without speaking to people in their daily lives.

Community support is so important, not just for the vulnerable in our society, but for people of all ages and stages across the spectrum to truly thrive. We all need connection in one form or another, and for those involved the benefits are infinite. As the restrictions eased, despite the apprehension about gathering in groups, people yearned for face-to-face, in person social connection with one another. Community activities, workshops and events were reintroduced, enabling people to reconnect, entertain, celebrate, and enjoy a range of activities together.

As soon as it was safe to do so, the volunteer hosts with Chirpy Plus invited members of their communities on both sides of the Tasman to reconnect and enjoy social activities together again. Similarly, I offered a range of community workshops to bring individuals and groups back together to chat, share ideas and experiences, to participate in meaningful projects and learn with and from one another, and to have fun. And the great thing is, people were very receptive to the opportunity. I'm lucky to be doing something I love and believe in - I inspire people to do what inspires them. How awesome is that!

My advice to others, "***Every day counts so make the most of it. Life beyond the mid-point can be even more productive and fulfilling than what has gone before, depending on your mindset. Set new priorities, follow your passion, and take advantage of the opportunities around you***".

Through their life changing experiences, Denise Carnihan and Marie Hannan used their business savvy in New Zealand, to solve bigger problems – Denise in Kenya and Marie in the villages in Nepal. Through their businesses they provide education and meaningful work at a grass roots level, connection with the wider world, and hope for the future for these communities in terms of social, economic, and environmental change. Denise and Marie were not daunted by their experience, or their ideas. Quite the reverse. Their experience fuelled their conviction to take massive action and make a difference, with amazing results. How empowering is that for everyone concerned.

Balanced Lifestyle

Molly Burke (Second Act Services) is enjoying a bohemian lifestyle with her partner in Whanganui. Tapping into her creativity she is *"making magic"* in the community. When asked if she had advice to offer others, she recalled a story about a young talented friend and mentor of hers, named Mark, who died during the Aids epidemic in San Francisco. He had a mantra that he repeatedly sang like a Gregorian chant. Whenever the going gets tough she thinks about Mark and uses the chant, *"Oh what the f…. Go for it anyway! It works for me. Whenever I share this, it keeps him close in my heart and part of him lives on"*.

Molly also believes, *"You don't have to start a business as we would have done it in our 20's or 30's, when we thought we had all the time in the world. In the second half of life, we have limited time to waste. It's important to manage our energy levels and give ourselves permission to work less, enjoy what we do, and have more work-life balance. The fabulous thing is that when we do this, younger people will notice, and they will see that they can do this too"*.

Heather Knewstubb (Time Genie) said, *"I started my own business for the same reason that hundreds of people do. I wanted an interesting job, working with interesting people - without having to commute an hour each way into the city. My work with creative clients is interesting and working from home also gives me more time to enjoy the wonderful lifestyle."*

Like Heather, Tom Rodden enjoys a balanced lifestyle, and is excited about what the future holds for his business Peak Coaching.   His advice to business owners, *"Plan to exit your business. It's a 2–5-year process to make it happen. We can work through it. Don't leave it to chance"*.

Now in their mid-70's Judith and Ken Shilling are planning to step away from their thriving businesses and are looking to sell. They are going to try a new venture called 'retirement'. Ken is looking forward to being more involved in Rotary, join an organisation like the MenzShed, and increase fitness with more time on his bike -

not electric. Judith who is involved with Inner Wheel, is looking forward to spending more of her time in the community.

It takes courage, fortitude, and a tolerance for risk to become an entrepreneur at any age. Whilst most of us want flexibility and autonomy in our work, setting up and operating a business requires a high degree of confidence and enthusiasm, a wide range of skills, it is time consuming, and is generally harder than working for someone else.

It's evident that it's never too late to change gears, consider new options, possibilities, and adventures, or get started on what you secretly wanted to do, and clearly more and more people in the second half of life are choosing to go down this path. The entrepreneurs who feature in this book show us that the opportunities are limitless. They are all excited about the path they have chosen and the lifestyle they have created for themselves. They are an integral part of Aotearoa New Zealand's thriving economy and an asset to their community. Energised with what they have accomplished, they look forward to what the future holds.

11 Afterthoughts

A huge debt of gratitude is due to the 33 awesome entrepreneurs at 50+ who generously shared their stories with me over the past three years and good-naturedly, and without complaint, wondered what the heck had happened to the project during, and in the wake of, the pandemic. In response to the nature and scale of the crisis, every aspect of our lives drastically changed, literally overnight. Everything in our lives came to a grinding halt for weeks, or months at a time depending on where individuals were located and the nature of their business. An extended period of uncertainty ensued, while we all lived through the 'anticipate', 'start', 'pivot', and 'stop again' process of the 'new normal' cycle. Small businesses were extremely vulnerable, and for this reason the project was put on hold for what seemed like an age. For those involved, I appreciate your patience. It's been an honour to have chatted with you, and a privilege to be able to share your stories with others.

Individuals who choose to become entrepreneurs in midlife or beyond, challenge the stereotypical belief, that advancing age narrows down life choices. It doesn't. The desire to develop and utilise our skills, set new priorities, accomplish new things, generate an income, and have a positive impact within our communities or the wider world grows stronger with age. The entrepreneurs showcased in this book, are living examples of what can be achieved. It is possible to generate an income while crafting a life of independence and purpose .... if you want to.

There is rarely an isolated reason why people change gears and embark on entrepreneurial activity in the second half of life, but there is a trigger – a spark, or a combination of experiences that signals that it's time to change direction and sets off a chain of events. This could be as simple as a conversation, or a set of circumstances that presents a challenge, highlights an issue or an opportunity, initiates an idea and stimulates the motivation to do something about it. While everyone's story is different, none of these individuals accepted the status quo. They all set off on a journey to explore what they really wanted to do. Through these stories we learned their compelling reason for starting their businesses – their **'WHY'**, after which they set to work to create their own reality.

The nature of the businesses that are showcased in this book are many and varied. Some service the domestic market, others operate on a global scale. While most of the people who feature in this book are micropreneurs, others are serial entrepreneurs who run two or more businesses simultaneously, or successively, one after another. And there are the social entrepreneurs, who work to resolve a particular issue in the community – whether in New Zealand or overseas, or help others to develop skills, and/or build resilience and cohesion, while also generating an income. We learned how these entrepreneurs started their ventures, what motivates them and how their business ideas, skills and experience evolved over time. We observed their resilience in response to the challenges they faced, and we gained insight into their aspirations for the future. What's more, these individuals were willing to offer their words of wisdom and encouragement with you, and fundamental tips and techniques were shared along the way.

It's never too late to change direction. We can change gears at any time if we want to, depending on our mindset. If you have that itchy feeling of 'what's next for me', and are willing to expand your horizons, inspired by their example, you might like to 'give it a go' and start your own business too.

Enjoy the adventure.

Business Directory

Annette Burrell   The Inner Path | Be your true self | Feel alive and happy

Denise Carnihan   www.kailanipearl.com and Home (helpinghandafricatours.com)

Cliff Gott   www.securetime.nz

Jan Thornborough   jan.thornborough@intelligensia.co.nz

Helen Hancox   www.facebook.com/HelenGlenysHancox

Anne Russell and Rosemary Emery www.offthepage.co.nz

Suz Stokes 35 Day Detox - The Natural Detox for YOUR Mind, Body & Soul.

Richard Eltherington   Healthy Start Group

Andrew Burn   www.ERP365.NZ

Jules Fitzgerald   www.facebook.com/julia.fitzgerald.35

Kareen Holland   Organic Skincare | KD One New Zealand Natural Beauty

Genevieve McLachlan Genevieve McLachlan | Facebook and Official Site of doTERRA New Zealand | dōTERRA Essential Oils

Tom Rodden Peak Coaching | How prepared is your business for sale?

Tony Yuile Tony Yuile HypnoCoach - IBS IBS hypnotherapy and

Your Life Live It (thinkific.com)

Cathy Sheppard   Your People Experts | BSI People Skills

Mark and Sone Edwards   Home | Sone's Sauces (sonessauces.com)

Raewynne Graf   https://atahu.nz

Karen Radford and Stephen Sexton www.dri-sleeper.com

Jeanie Morrison-Low   www.kapitihearing.co.nz

John Skene   John Skene - Aviation History Advocate - Aviation Tales (aviation-tales.com)

Phil Byrne Eco Couriers, Shifters, Movers Kapiti, Levin, Porirua - Eco Shifter

Marie Hannan   Nepal NZ Connection | Facebook

Carol and Shaun Mahoney   About Us - Chirpy Plus NZ

Molly Burke COVID-19 | Second Act Services/career change (mollyburke.net)

Liz Koh Enrich Retirement - Retirement Education, Revolutionised

Heather Knewstubb   www.timegenie.co.nz

Paul Streekstra   www.birdsongaudio.com

Ken and Judith Shilling   www.tisco.net.nz and www.linktechnology.net

Angela Robertson   www.angelarobertson.nz/resources/

Thank You

Thank you for reading **'Changing Gears – Entrepreneurs at 50+'**. I hope you enjoyed it. I'd really appreciate it if you would take a few minutes to provide a review of this book, whether positive or negative as reviews help other readers to find books that would be of interest to them.

By the same author

The ***'Older and Bolder'*** series

Available from your favourite online bookstores in paperback, Kindle, and e-book formats

Life on Our Own Terms

Celebrating Life on Our Own Terms

Embracing Life on Our Own Terms

Creating Life on Our Own Terms

Dr Angela C Robertson (books2read.com)

Want to be kept up to date with new books, information, and speaking engagements? If so, email me Kiaora@angelarobertson.nz to register your interest and be one of the first to find out about new releases.

For more information and details of events check out my website www.angelarobertson.nz

ABOUT THE AUTHOR

Dr Angela Robertson is an author, inspirational speaker, and workshop facilitator with more than 40 years' experience in adult and community development. She inspires and supports individuals of all ages to maximise their potential to enhance the quality of their lives, work, and relationships.

In her work with individuals, groups, and communities she encourages people to broaden their perspective on ageing, continually expand their horizons, take advantage of the opportunities around them and channel their energy into activities that matter. Through her workshops she helps individuals to create living legacies, connecting communities of people to future generations.